TALES OF THE
EAST COAST
from the Thames to the Wash

Frank Tice

IAN HENRY PUBLICATIONS

© Frank Tice, 1995

ISBN 0 86025 464 X

NOR:PA
Dedicated to the memory of
my wife
with gratitude for
58 happy years together

The illustration on the cover is of
Woodbridge Tide Mill

Printed by
Watkiss Studios, Ltd.
Holmes Court, Biggleswade, Bedfordshire SG18 9ST
for
Ian Henry Publications, Ltd.
20Park Drive, Romford, Essex RM1 4LH

THE ESSEX COAST

Where does the River Thames end and the North Sea begin? Traditionally the Crowstone at Leigh marks the boundary of the jurisdiction of the City of London on the river, while the Port of London Authority now says that an imaginary line drawn from Havengore Creek in Essex to Warden Point in the Isle of Sheppey `marks the spot'.

However, our coastal journey begins a few miles upstream where Tilbury was known all over the world to those "who go down to the sea in ships". The nearest of the Docks of the Port of London Authority to the sea, its miles of quays and landing stages can accommodate vessels of every kind.

There are three historical events connected with Tilbury not to be forgotten.

The Venerable Bede (673-735), in his monumental *History of the English Church and People* (completed 731), has placed on record the fact that it was from Tilbury that Bishop Cedd organised the first Christian Mission to the East Saxons; "Sigbert ... King of the East Saxons ... asked Oswy to send teachers to convert his people to the Faith of Christ, and baptize them. Accordingly the King sent to the province of the Middle Angles and summoned the man of God, Cedd, whom he dispatched to evangelize the East Saxons ... Bishop Finan ... consecrated Cedd Bishop of the East Saxons ... Cedd built churches in several places ... especially in Ythancaster (the Roman `Orthona') and that place called Tileburgh (Tilbury). More will be said about Ythancaster as this history unfolds.

The second event is much more widely known. In the days when England was expecting to be attacked by the Spanish Armada, the forces of Queen Elizabeth gathered at Tilbury to ensure that if the Spaniards did get past Drake, they would not enter the Thames to reach London. On the 8th August, 1588, the Queen came to address them. The troops were all volunteers, there being no 'regular' army and, after praising them with the words "Let tyrants fear" and alluding to her reliance upon "... the loyal hearts and good-will of my subjects", she is credited with making the following declaration:

"I know I have but the body of a weak and feeble woman, but I have the heart and stomach of a king, and of a King of England too! I think foul scorn that any Prince of Europe should dare to invade the borders of my realm."

The third incident recalls the hectic days of 1648, and the Civil War. Lord Fairfax, having conferred with Cromwell at the pargeted Sun Inn at Saffron Waldon, was recruiting cavalry in various parts of Essex, preparatory to leading them in the Seige of Colchester. He called a halt at West Tilbury where, to ensure their safety, especially from marauding bands of cattle thieves, the horses were stabled in St James's Church.

+++

The story of human occupation of the site which is now Leigh-on-Sea goes back through the ages. Pre-historic man had settlements here; the Romans occupied the area; and Saxons and Normans followed in their turn.

By 1553 Leigh had become a naval base, several Elizabethan men-of-war being moored at the quay. In the 17th century when the Dutchman, Van Tromp, attempted to sweep the English Fleet from the seas, the importance of Leigh's strategic position was increased; Admiral Blake used its facilities to re-fit his fleet.

Tradition has it that the *Mayflower* was built at Leigh. No-one can be certain that this was so, but even those who doubt agree that she must have called there to take in provisions, as the flour which she carried was known to have been milled at Billericay .

Oysters have had their breeding grounds on certain parts of the Essex coast since before the time when the Romans lived ashore. Colchester Oyster Fishery, off Mersea Island, is the most famous centre for their cultivation today, but at one time Leigh had its oyster beds as well. Unfortunately, the pollution of the waters of the Thames caused the oysters to die away, and that particular fishery was abandoned. However, the gathering of other shell-fish such as cockles, mussels, whelks and winkles has continued to provide an industry for local people. The specially designed boats used by the local fishermen, known as 'Leigh Bawleys', will go down into history, not only for the specific work for which they were designed, but also for their heroic participation in the rescue of the British Expeditionary Force from the beaches of Dunkirk in 1940.

Southend-on-Sea has a reputation for mud: its famous Pier, over a mile long, was constructed to carry people from the Promenade to the pleasure steamers lying off in deep water at the time of low tide. The pier end was partially destroyed by fire in 1976, but has since been re-built. It suffered yet another fire, this time at the shore end, in June, 1995. Being the nearest seaside place to London, thousands of people visit the town every year; to cater for them and entertain them was the town's chief occupation. The Promenade stretches for seven miles from Chalkwell to Shoeburyness, the busiest part being near the Pier in Southend. The establishment of the modern resort came about because the 'South End' of the mother village of Prittlewell found popularity after it received the patronage of Royalty in the person of the infant Princess Charlotte and her mother, Princess Caroline of Brunswick.

+++

The first recorded name of Foulness was 'Fughelness', christened by the Romans 'The Isle of Birds'. Later corrupted to 'Foulness', this island is the 'toe' of Essex; the eastern extremity of the Hundred of Rochford.

This low headland, a black, flat, almost treeless area, has seen the coming and going of men for thousands of years; and it would appear that preparations for war have never been long absent from their activities. The primitive workshops of Stone Age men, Roman kilns, and the defensive earthworks thrown up by the Danes, as they retreated from the forces of King Alfred, all tell their own story. These historic sites are located in some six

St Mary the Virgin, Foulness, after the 1953 floods

thousand acres of marshland - but cannot be visited by the public as the area is in the hands of the military and closed to civilians. Foulness is a secret place, and always has been. Smugglers knew it and used it; and during the Crimean War thousands of Russian prisoners were herded together in its bleak solitude. Many of them died of ague and were buried in long-forgotten mass graves.

But the Ness has not a legacy of war alone. In 1386 the 'Chapel of Ease' was in the presentation of Lady Joan de Bohun, and, after her, the Lords of the Manor. The Chapel being so slenderly provided for financially, the Cure was administered by a Chantry Priest, who was charged with the duty of performing all the Offices for the inhabitants who, on account of infirmities or even 'overflowing tides', were often unable to attend worship in their own Parish Churches at Rochford, Sutton, Shopland or the Wakerings. On the dissolution of the Chantries in 1554 the Chapel was made into a Parish Church.

One Rector was Arthur Dent, a Puritan, who wrote a book called *A Plain Man's Pathway to Heaven*, which had a deep and lasting spiritual effect upon John Bunyan. Bunyan's first wife brought it with her on her marriage to the cottage at Elstow, and Bunyan wrote: "I would read with her, and in the book I found things that were pleasing to me". Published in the early days of the establishment of the Rectory at Foulness, Dent's book became so popular that it reached its 24th edition in 1637. There is one legend concerning the island worth recording; in his *Worthies of Essex*, Dr. Fuller says that in 1648 an army of mice shaved off all the grass at the roots, which withered and became infectious to cattle. The following March flocks of owls flew in and destroyed the mice.

+++

The River Crouch is the southern border of the Hundred of Dengie; and is well known because of the small town of Burnham standing upon its banks. The town is a balanced mixture of the old and the new. Modern buildings have been erected alongside the old; Georgian and Victorian architecture can still be seen, while the distinctive weatherboarded cottages are almost inevitable in such an Essex environment.

The parish occupies the south-eastern extremity of Dengie, where the River Crouch discharges into the sea. Its history began at an unknown date before the Conquest, the 'Lands' being held by Aluuart, a 'freeman'. At Domesday they formed part of the possessions of Ralph Baynard, who had 'taken' the lands of Aluuart and nine other freemen. The Church was given by Walter Fitz-Robert to the Priory at Dunmow, and a Vicarage, erected before 1243, was confirmed in its Rights in the year of its foundation by the Dean and Chapter of Saint Paul's Cathedral.

The River Crouch is an example of extremes. Above the tidal waters it attracts little attention; but the estuary, in terms of navigational possibilities, is probably the finest on the whole of England's East Coast. Well may Burnham be known as 'the Cowes of East Anglia', for this is a premier centre for sailing. In summer the town is thronged with those who love 'messing about in boats', and the waters of the estuary are crowded with craft of every description.

The Dengie Marshes are a great expanse of mud-flats and saltings inhabited by wildlife of the larger species, including the bittern, the curlew and the fox.

The word 'Dengie' is eloquent of the history of England a thousand years ago. This was the bleak land invaded by the Danes, sailing their longships lordly up the creeks and estuaries with the flag of Odin flying and their wild blood-curdling War Cry carried far upon the wind. They landed, raided, robbed and slew. When eventually most of them withdrew, some remained, married local girls and settled down. So the area became 'Dane's Ey' - 'Dane's Island' - 'Dengie'. Evidence of their coming and settlement can be seen even today in the tall bony frame, the blond hair and the blue eyes of some of the real local native inhabitants: physical traces of ancestry never really die out.

The ownership of the Dengie Marshes at the time of Edward the Confessor was invested in one named Siric; at the Survey they

St Nicholas, Tillingham

St Thomas, Bradwell-juxta-mare

7

belonged to Odo, Bishop of Bayeux, adjoining lands being the property of the Abbey of St Valéry in Picardy. In succeeding years the estate passed through many hands; at one time it was given by the Crown to the Hospital of the Savoy in the Strand, London; a Hospital suppressed in 1551 by Edward VI. Edward granted the Manor of Dengie to the Dean and Chapter of St Paul's Cathedral, but changed it in 1553 to the Mayor and Commonalty of London. After that it passed into private ownership.

Southminster is the largest village in the Marshes, while Asheldham and Tillingham stand on sites of ancient settlements too old to date.

Tillingham stands on rising ground above the level of the marshes. Ethelbert, King of Kent, gave the lands of this parish to the Church of St. Paul in the City of London, of which he was the Founder; and ever since the ownership has been vested in the Dean and Chapter of the Cathedral. The village is a pleasant place, a collection of charming cottages, their beauty emphasised particularly by one long, white-timbered dwelling which stands by the Churchyard gate. This is made even more lovely in the summer when the trailing roses are in bloom.

On the north-eastern corner of Dengie Hundred, in the midst of an ancient solitude there lies a lonely peninsula, a land of marshes, keen east winds and slimy black mud. Here the River Blackwater, on whose banks stands the ancient town of Maldune (Maldon), runs into the North Sea at Blackwater Bay, which is the *Fluvius Idumanius* of the Romans. In this desolate spot stands the village of Bradwell - the addition of `juxta mare' [`next to the sea'] being given to distinguish it from Bradwell near Coggeshall.

Domesday records the name as `Effecestre' formed of two syllables, `Effe' or `Offe', a contraction of `Othona' and `Cestre', generally affixed by the Saxons to names of places where there had been a Roman camp or station.

The Roman fort and settlement here was `Othona'; known by the Saxons as `Ythancaster', as already mentioned in this record in connection with Tilbury. The Venerable Bede, in his

Ecclesiastical History (Ch. XXII Bk. III) says: "Cedd built a church in the city which, in the language of the Saxons is called Ythancaster". Ralph Niger, `the Monk of Coggeshall', also refers to the place by the same name. All that remains of Othona today are extensive `footings' covered over by agricultural cultivation and one small outcrop of Roman wall, almost hidden by trees and brambles entangled among the undergrowth, which has to be pulled away before any of the ancient stonework can be seen.

A visitor to the village of Bradwell-juxta-Mare, wandering out of the main street and down a path through the fields toward the sea, came upon what he thought to be an old barn, in use by a farmer for the storage of fodder for his cattle. More curious than others who had been there before him, he closely examined the building, noting its unusual height, the well shaped stones and the Roman bricks and tiles which had been used in its construction. He was particularly attracted by the high gables and the signs that there had been arches at one end. He measured, and excavated, and discovered the remains of a porch on the western side and an apse on the east. These, and other relevant discoveries convinced him that he had stepped right back into history, to the time of the Saxons living on the site of the old Roman fort of Othona. The building which he had taken to be a barn was, in fact, the church built by Bishop Cedd in the 7th century.

In his monumental *Historica* the Venerable Bede tells the story of St Peter ad Murum: he writes

"About this time - 653 - the East Saxons who had rejected the Faith, again accepted it, and Sighert their king asked Oswy, King of Northumbria, to send teachers to convert his people and to baptize them.

Accordingly the King sent the man of God, Cedd, to evangelize the East Saxons. Cedd built a Church in the city which the Saxons called Ythancaster."

Think of the irony of the situation! The occupying Roman forces built a string of fortifications, `The Count of the Saxon Shore', from the Wash to the Solent, to repel attacks from would-

The chapel of St Peter ad Murum

be Saxon invaders. One of these forts was Othona on the salt marshes of the Essex coast. When Cedd arrived he found a Saxon community living among the derelict remains of the fort which had been built to keep them away!

For the foundations of Cedd's Church they used the twelve feet thick walls of the Roman fort. For the walls they utilised the stones, thin red Roman tiles, and the bricks from the former building which were scattered about the ruins. Today Cedd's Church still stands as one of the oldest Church buildings surviving in the land; a consecrated building; the Citadel of Christ athwart the citadel of Caesar.

The Church of St Peter-ad-Murum, anciently named 'Capella de la Val', has not been entirely ignored. In 1442 an enquiry was instituted into its true purpose, and a Jury 'found' that " ... it had a chancel a nave and a small tower with two bells : that it was burnt, and repaired by the Rector and the parishioners". Later, in 1821, a report published by Thomas Wright in his *History of Essex* stated that "... some remains of the building have been made to form part of a barn." After the discovery of its true character Bradwell's 'Chapel on the Salting's edge' was fully restored and re-consecrated by the first Bishop of Chelmsford in 1920.

A map of this part of the Essex coast or an aerial photograph shows this estuary to be the most conspicuous break in the land-line. Over two miles wide at Sales Point, the river is a busy water way, although treacherous by reason of shoals and capricious tides. Like the Crouch, the river's upper reaches, in this case above Maldon, are so inconspicuous that their existence may be missed altogether. Dr. Marcus Cox in his *Little Guide to Essex* says that it is fed by the Podsbrook, the old name for the Brain, which enters the Blackwater at Witham. In its early stages the river is known as the Pant, to be seen as a sturdy 'youngster' as it crosses the village green in the beautiful and much-visited village of Finchingfield. This was the old name for the river, used by Bede, but the importance of the Blackwater today lies in the fact the modern and busy town of Maldon lies near its entry into the sea.

Maldon has old and famous places; old houses which over-hang the streets, an inn built in the 14th century and showing unmistakable signs of being altered in some way in every century since, a vicarage with ancient doorways and mediæval paintings, the Old Moot Hall, and one of the best preserved fragments of an Abbey in East Anglia.

Maldon's `Finest Hour' belongs to an event a thousand years ago. The *Anglo-Saxon Chronicle* records for the year 991: "This year was Brithnorth slain at Maldron [*sic*]". Little further information on the subject would have been available had it not been for the survival of a manuscript with a description of *The Battle of Maldon*. If it is not an eye-witness account of the battle, the way in which it is written makes it clear that it was compiled from the accounts furnished by eye-witnesses.

The poem tells how the invading Danish horde led by Anlaf was encamped when the East Anglian ealdorman Byrhtnoth (another form of spelling) arrived with an army. A battle ensued in which Byrhtnoth was killed and the defeat of the English was total. Professor Freeman's translation of the poem begins with a description of the first clash of the opposing forces:

> Waded then the slaughter-wolves,
> For water they cared not,
> The Viking Host
> There 'gainst the fierce ones
> Ready was standing
> Brithnorth with his warriors.
> Then let them from their hands
> The pile-hard spears,
> The sharply grounded
> Javelins fly;
> Bows were busy,
> Shields the point received,
> Bitter was the sword-rush;
> Warriors fell.

But, as Brithnorth dies, he stands and thanks God:
> Yet a word quoth
> The hoary war-man;
> The daring youths
> Bade he gang forth,
> His good companions.
> He to Heaven looked :
> Thank Thee, Nation's wielder,
> For all good things
> That I in world have bode.
> Now I own, mild Maker,
> That I most have need
> That Thou to my ghost
> Good should grant,
> That my soul to Thee
> Now may make its way.

This poem is significant because it is the first example of English 'Battle Poetry' in which the hero dies with a Christian cry upon his lips.

To historians, the town of Maldon is known as the main Essex port in mediæval times, as the scene of this epic battle and as the oldest Borough in Essex. In modern times the town is cherished by the water-sportsman, because, next to Burnham, it is the principal yachting centre in the county and the base for the sailing barges which make such a fine spectacle when they go out upon the tide.

Thames Sailing Barges were remarkable craft. They were not built in the conventional style with seams that could be caulked: the hull was made of two layers of one-and-a-half inch pitchpine planking, with a mixture of tar and cow or elk hair between, and rabbeted seams. Their average length was eighty-five to ninety feet, and they could carry a cargo of up to one-hundred-and-thirty tons. The main mast was seventy feet high, and they had five sails; mainsail, topsail, foresail, staysail and mizzen. The mainsail alone weighed over one ton, and all sails, with the exception of the staysail, were dressed with a mixture of red and yellow ochre and fish oil.

These barges were crewed by `a man and a boy', or sometimes by a man and his wife, "...born to a life of toil and physical struggle".

In the second half of the 19th century there were about four thousand of these vessels in service, but their commercial value declined through the years, until they disappeared from the scene. The inevitable revival came, however, when people began to re-discover their beauty, power and operative perfection; as has happened with vintage motor cars and aeroplanes. Then they became the rich man's plaything; and most of the activity is centred at Maldon.

+++

Between the rivers Blackwater and Colne lies an extensive area of marshland, veined with water. It is a wide waste-ground, battled for by both land and sea; stubbornly maintained by the former, yet subject to incessant incursions from the latter. At high tide it has the appearance of a vast surface of moss floating on the sea, with patches of shining water traversing in all directions. The creeks, some of considerable length, are as arteries from which branch out a fibrous tissue of smaller channels. At noon-tides, and especially at the equinoctial periods, the sea asserts itself over the whole region, overflowing the whole area, leaving the island of Mersea alone standing out of the flood.

A more desolate region can scarcely be conceived, yet it is not without its beauty. In summer-time the thrift mantles the marshes with the appearance of shot-silk: after that a purple glow steals over the waste as the sea lavender bursts into flower, and every creek-pool and bank is fringed with the blossom of the wild sea aster. Later still in the year the glasswort turns to carmine.

The marshes are alive with wild-fowl; sea-mews and crows, wild duck and grey geese, the stately heron wades in the pools and swans abound. The plaintive piping of the curlew can be heard, as also can the `barking' of the brent geese as they return each

November from their breeding places in the far North.

The island of Mersea lies at the junction of the rivers Colne and Blackwater, forming an estuary where they both discharge into the sea. It is parted from the mainland by the Pyefleet Channel, and retains a name closely resembling the original Saxon, 'Meres-ig' - meaning 'The Island of the Sea'. The only access to the island from the mainland is by a causeway called the 'Strood' crossing the Pyefleet Creek and, although this has been re-constructed several times, the roadway is still often covered by the sea at high tides.

The Strood is the setting for an apparition which has been reported and discussed for many generations, and still is today. It is said that if one walks across the Strood at midnight when the moon is at the full, you will hear following, the footsteps of a Roman soldier who has patrolled its length every night since it was first built.

Other visitants are also said to have made appearances in these parts. Take, for example, the story told by an old Mersea fisher-man who could neither read nor write. He lived in a shack which he had built for himself from ship's timbers and had never been more than a mile or two from the island and therefore had never seen a railway train. This was his story: "Oi lay in me bed a-lookin' outer me winder. Bright moon that was, bright as day, an' Oi saw an owd feller what stood six foot. He had a leather jerkin on wi' a belt an' cross gaiters under the knees. He had a sword an' a funny owd hat wi' wings an' a beard."

How is that for a traditional description of a Viking warrior, from one who had never seen a picture or read a book?

Another Mersea man, who was persuaded to tell his story on the radio, created a great deal of interest. He said that one night he was out on the marshes after wildfowl, and he saw 'a giant of a man come down from the sea wall, stride over the creek, and go walking away in the mist'.

It was stories like these that prompted W H Ogilvie to write
On every moon-lit roadway, down every starry lane,

Forgotten hoofs make music, lost wagons creak and strain;
The mantling mists of moonlight half hides and half
    reveals
The glitter of pale harness, the curve of shadowy wheels.

Mersea Island was unquestionably occupied by the Romans, and from some of their personal possessions which antiquarians have discovered buried in the island's soil, it is believed that here was the `seat' of a Roman General of considerable importance.

Among other relics, a mosaic pavement, twenty feet square, was discovered two centuries ago; and in a small tiled underground chamber, a casket was discovered which contained a glass bowl holding the ashes of a Roman, whose body had been cremated in the 1st century A.D.. Men digging near the parish church exposed foundations very similar in shape to a six-spoke wheel, which may have been the base of a monument, the footings of a tower, or even the site of a lighthouse.

During the invasions of this country by the Danes, Mersea was frequently the landing-place and retreat of their ferocious bands; and King Alfred the Great besieged a large party of them here some time in the year 894.

The *Anglo-Saxon Chronicle* states that in the following year, 895, some of the Danes from Mersea towed their ships up the River Lea as far as Hertford. In this way they attempted to form a `pincer movement' to encircle the City of London: while at the same time others of their number sailed up the Thames to attack the City from that side. To prevent a recurrence, and to thwart the designs of the attackers, Hertford Castle was built to defend London's `back door'.

Defence was of paramount importance in the early days of the habitation of Mersea Island. A small fortification was erected at the south-east corner of the island, to defend the estuary of the River Colne. Its importance was emphasised when Parliamentarian Forces seized it during the Seige of Colchester in 1648 and thus effectively cut off sea-borne relief from the town. Later, during the wars which England fought against the Dutch a camp was reestablished on the site to prevent the enemy from landing.

The island is divided into two parishes named in accordance with their respective positions - East Mersea and West Mersea. Formerly a smuggler's paradise, West is now a popular holiday resort, with modern beach huts and chalets struggling along the fringe of the shore. East is primarily a fishing and sailing community, with a distinctive `not-to-be-hurried' atmosphere.

Reference has been made to the Pyefleet Channel, the Creek separating Mersea Island from the mainland. From there and other places around the island's coast, come the famous `Colchester Natives', bred in the grounds belonging to the Colne Oyster Fishery. The Season is `opened' by the Mayor of Colchester going to sea (not far!), and making what is traditionally the `first catch'. This ceremony is followed by the grandiose Colchester Oyster Feast, held in the Colchester Town Hall, attended by representatives of Church and State from a wide area.

The oyster fishery has always formed a unique and valuable part of the commercial life of Colchester. Richard I granted the burgesses of Colchester the right to the fishing in the River Colne, a grant confirmed by subsequent charters, especially that of Edward IV. The fishery thus detailed consisted not only of the River Colne itself, but included all creeks and waters with which the river communicates; that is to say, the whole area or stretch which is sometimes designated `Colne Water'. While the burgesses of Colchester were granted "...The full, sole and absolute power to take and dispose of all the oysters within the said river", the inhabitants of other parishes adjoining the water - Brightlingsea, Wivenhoe, and East Donyland - were "... allowed to fish therein by license from the Mayor".

+++

Brightlingsea is the only town north of the Thames to be a member of the Brotherhood of the Cinque Ports: it was a `limb' of the Kentish town and port of Sandwich; and, in common with other member towns, provided ships for the Fleet during the wars of the Middle Ages. Its main business is still building and

17

repairing boats; together with yachting, a sport increasing in popularity year by year.

Before the Conquest the Lordship was retained by the Crown, but was given by the Conqueror to Eudo Dapifer, William's steward, who was responsible for the building of Colchester Castle. Eudo made this Manor part of the Endowment of St John's Abbey in Colchester which he had built at his own expense. At the Dissolution it was granted to Thomas Cromwell, upon whose attainer it returned to the Crown. In 1576 Queen Elizabeth surrendered it to private hands.

At one time the parish, with the exception of the road to Thorington, was almost surrounded by water, from the sea and from the River Colne and its tributaries; a fact which led Speed to suppose that this was the island to which the Danes fled after their defeat by King Alfred: but succeeding historians have proved that this opinion is erroneous, and have substantiated the claim of Mersea Island to be the place of retreat.

From Brightlingsea's broad street, in which stands the modern Church, many narrow streets lead down to the quay. The old parish church surmounts a hill-top over a mile away inland, its high tower forming a landmark for miles by land and sea. It is a noble building, standing among tall pines, and speaks of the wealthy merchants and humble seamen who dwelt in the town and were buried here centuries ago

+++

At Colne Point there begins the Nature Reserve of the Essex Naturalist's Trust. A notice board reads: "Beware of Adders; if bitten, go at once to Colchester Hospital". Adders there may be and, if so, they should be avoided, but this is certainly one way of persuading unwanted visitors from entering the area.

Here also begins another stretch of typical sea-level East Anglian coast line. There are beaches of deep, soft sand, guarded on the landward side by a barricade of dunes separating the sea from the marshy region inland. These dunes or sand-hills did not develop casually, but are the result of a carefully engineered plan to encourage their formation as a means of coastal defence. Their existence depends entirely upon the marram grass which has been planted along the beaches to stabilise the shifting sand and so to form a barrier against the waves.

When beach sand dries it becomes so powdery that it is scattered by the wind: if this were allowed to go on unchecked all the top sand would be scoured away and the area flooded by the first abnormal tide. The answer to this problem was found in marram grass, a prolific form of vegetation which thrives on barren sand, sending its roots down to form a fibrous 'matting' below the surface, thus knitting together the foundations of the beach. The grass grows rapidly, and as the light sand is blown by the wind hillocks are formed among the grass until in time a 'wall' is constructed. Other plant life, such as bindweed and sea holly grows among the grass, and eventually meadow grass and moss appears, and together they go a long way toward stopping the incursion of the waves.

It may be well at this point to emphasise how important it is that visitors should not damage the marram grass, particularly its roots. Those who go among it to picnic or to change into their bikinis, or to tell a girl-friend what lovely eyes she has (and all these things do take place in the grass) should be careful not to do anything to endanger the defences against the sea.

For the next hundred miles or so, with the exception of a few cliffs, the coast is flat and low, and is largely defended from the waters by dunes, in this way.

Another type of grass important in the defence against encroachment by the sea is *Spartina Townsendii*, which, although out of the geographical sequence of this coastal description, may be mentioned here. *Spartina* builds up defences, not of sand, but of mud. The story of this plant is interesting. About 1850 a species of *Spartina*, a kind of 'rice grass' of American origin, was found growing in the harbour at Poole, Dorset. Near the turn of the century, a distinctly new form of this plant appeared, which, being tall and robust, was obviously a hybrid of the American-

English grasses. Named *Spartina Townsendii* it was found that it could live and grow on soft mud, which previously had been devoid of all plant life. It also has the ability to retain silt, so raising the level of the mud bank. One condition appeared necessary to ensure its growth, it had to be covered and bared regularly by the action of the tides.

This grass proved its value in the estuary of the River Stour which divides Essex from Suffolk. In 1923 John Keeble of Brantham brought a truck load of these plants to set in the mud of the Stour at Cattawade, opposite to what was then the Xylonite Works. Within twenty years the upper estuary had big beds of grass, and the level of the mud had risen two feet.

The growth of *Spartina* is welcomed by land-drainage authorities and those responsible for maintaining the tidal banks, because the beds of the grass act as cushions upon which waves can expend some of their force before reaching the sea walls.

+++

Saint Osyth is a picturesque village, with groups of attractive cottages, gabled and half-timbered, and with traditional Essex weatherboard elevations and pantile roofs; some of them of considerable age. The site of the village was inhabited in pre-historic times, as flint instruments and other relics discovered there indicate. A mosaic pavement, together with Roman bricks used in the construction of certain buildings, prove that some of Cæsar's Legions knew the place as well. It is a village linked with both history and legend.

The true derivation of the Saxon name Chich is not known but that of Saint Osyth is from the daughter of Frithewald and Walburga, King and Queen of East Anglia (655-64), who were the first rulers to adopt the new Christian Faith. As soon as their daughter was old enough she was betrothed to Sigehere, son of Sigebert, the first Christian King of the neighbouring kingdom of the East Saxons (653-60).

Oysthia was born at Quarendon, but spent most of her child-hood with an aunt in Buckinghamshire. According to monkish legends she made a Vow of Virginity at an early age, but was compelled by her father to go through a marriage ceremony with Sigehere. Great festivities marked the wedding, but, when the feast was at its height, Sigehere saw a splendid stag in the open fields nearby and, without a thought for his bride, called his men together and went in pursuit. Osythia too left the feast and with her maids sought refuge in a nearby nunnery. The marriage was never consummated: Osythia took the Veil, and retired to the village of Chich, given to her at her wedding by her husband. Here she founded a church and established a Nunnery of Maturines of the Order of the Holy Trinity.

During one of the forays by the Danes, under the leadership of Inguar and Hubba, this religious establishment was plundered and partly destroyed and Osythia murdered. She was buried before the door of her church, but the *Anglo-Saxon Chronicles* state that later her remains were removed to Aylesbury. In an account of the burial places of English Saints, transcribed by Hicks from an old Saxon manuscript, it is said; "Next resteth Saint Osith, at Cice, near the sea, in St. Peter's monastery": it would therefore appear that, after resting at Aylesbury, the remains of Osythia were brought back to her own site and re-interred.

Osythia became recognised as a Saint and Martyr and tradition has it that for ages after her martyrdom she wandered around in Nunn's Wood, carrying her head in her hands, performing miracles and curing disease. There is one official record relating to this belief.

When, at her second internment at Chich, the Relics of the Holy Virgin were deposited in a casket by Maurice, Bishop of London [c.1086], the attending Bishop of Rochester was cured of a severe malady with which he had been afflicted for years.

Tanner's *Notitia - Essex v. X* suggests that the Nunnery at St. Osyth was supposed to have been the most ancient monastic establishment in England, but the Danes destroyed it so completely that no trace of it appears in any records before the Conquest, or in Domesday Book.

After the Danes had obtained regal domination in England, Chich was given by King Canute to Godwin, Earl of Kent, who granted it to Christ Church, Canterbury: but by the time of Domesday it had been taken from Canterbury and belonged to the See of London. The Bishop of London held the Manorial Rights in 12th century and he built an Augustinian Priory in honour of Saint Osythia. The Bishop, Richard de Belmeis, died suddenly in January, 1127, and the Canons elected as their Abbot William de Corbeuil, who was Archbishop of Canterbury from 1123 to 1136. Large benefactions made the Priory one of the largest monastic institutions in Essex.

In the year 1168 Henry II granted the Abbot and Canons of St. Osyth a Charter giving them the right to `... free warren' in the surrounding lands, with the liberty to keep two harriers (*leporarios*) and four fox-hounds (*bracheros*) for hunting the hare and the fox. This is said to be the first time fox hunting is officially mentioned in England. Imagine those portly monks hunting a fox in Riddles Wood with two couples of hounds! They must have been somewhat indifferently mounted, as in the inventory compiled when the Priory was closed five horses were sold for only £5; one blind horse for three shillings and fourpence, and a lame horse for twelve pence.

Another Charter granted them a Free Fair or Market, but this was annulled in 1317 on a `presentment' from Colchester "... that the Abbot of St Osyth held a market in the village EVERY SUNDAY to the great injury of the Town of Colchester". Further troubles ensued! Not content with hunting the hare and the fox and trading in a bazaar on Sundays, an Abbot in the reign of Richard II was imprisoned in Colchester Gaol for transgressing the `Forest Laws' and killing the King's Venison. For monks and friars who preferred the gentler sports there was excellent fishing in the lake at Nun's Wood. There is a legend that this wood was a favourite resort of Osythia herself in earlier times: it is even suggested that she was enjoying the sport of the rod when the Danes, landing at the creek close by found her and chopped off her head. It is further said that where her head fell there sprung up a fountain of tears and in order that the consequent stream might flow for ever in her memory; the monks directed it through a long pipe, passing the end through the centre of a tall, upright effigy, from which the tearful waters returned to earth again.

Where is this effigy and fountain now?

Its non-existence is 'explained' by the story that a man, wanting ballast for his yacht dug up and used the pipes, and thus destroyed the memorial of ages. It is a wonder that the yacht sailed with such desecrated ballast, because another legend avers that in Oysthia's day a sailor tore down and stole a piece of marble from the portico of her Church, "... and the boat in which it was placed remained as immovable as if it had been fixed to the earth, until the marble had been restored to the church from which it had been taken "

When trying, without success, to find the fountain, the poet George Crabbe wrote in 1790:

> The Holy Spring is turned aside,
> The arch is gone, the stream is dried;
> The plough has levelled all around,
> And here is now no Holy Ground.

In Abbot Vyntoner's time (he died in 1533), the greater part of the Priory buildings were demolished and re-built; the Gateway Abbot's Tower and other conventual buildings which remain today were of that period. The Gateway is panelled in bands of ashlar and flints, and has been described as one of the finest examples of monastic architecture in England. The Bishop's Lodging, although altered in 1865, retains a beautiful oriel and some fine interior panelling while the inner mansion, the building of which was commenced by Abbot John Vantoner in 1527, and enlarged by the D'Arcy family after the Reformation, has a handsome triple gateway and another beautiful oriel. The chequerwork clock tower and the Abbot's Tower are notable, as is also the Chapel, dating from the 14th century, having a vaulted ceiling of great beauty, supported on marble columns.

After Vyntoner's death his successor, Abbot Wetherick, subscribed to the King's supremacy and on 20th July, 1539, the Priory was surrendered to the King.

There followed a sequence of unseemly struggles among high officials for possession of the property. One who wanted it but could not get it was Lord Audley who secured the Abbey at [Saffron] Walden instead; on the site of which the mansion Audley End was built. He struggled hard for St Osyth before admitting defeat; even trying the unblushing devise of petty disparagement by writing to Cromwell and saying: "St Osyes standyth in the mersches, not very holsom, so that few of reputation, as I thynke, will kepe continual house in eny of it".

Cromwell, however, was well acquainted with the Priory and notwithstanding the "... unholsom merches", had decided to have it for himself.

Who was this Cromwell? Thomas Cromwell (not to be confused with the Protector), was the son of a blacksmith of Putney; he entered the service of Cardinal Wolsey (who was the son of a butcher in Ipswich) and was employed by the Cardinal in several important negotiations, including that of closing small monasteries which the Pope had granted to Wolsey for the foundation of his `New Colleges'.

When Wolsey fell, Cromwell found favour with Henry VIII and entered his service, where his rise to honours and distinction was even more rapid than that of his old master: but to what did it lead? The last advice of the fallen Cardinal to Thomas Cromwell was, according to Shakespeare;

> Let's dry our eyes; and thus far hear me, Cromwell;
> And - when I am forgotten, as I shall be;
> And sleep in dull cold marble, where no mention
> Of me more must be heard of - say, I taught thee
> Say, Wolsey - that once trod the ways of glory
> And sounded all the depths and shoals of honour,
> Found thee a way, out of the wreck, to rise in:
> A sure and safe one, though the master missed it.

St Osyth Priory; Abbot's Tower and Chapel

Mark but my fall, and that that ruin'd me.
Cromwell, I charge thee, fling away ambition;
By that sin fell the Angels."

(King Henry VIII)

How did Cromwell profit by this advice? In 1531 he became Secretary of State; next year Privy Councillor and Chancellor of the Exchequer; in 1536 Lord Privy Seal, Chancellor of the University of Cambridge and Lord Chamberlain. In the same year he was raised to the peerage as Lord Cromwell of Okeham and in 1540 he was made Earl of Essex and a Knight of the Garter.

But his fall came like a strike of lightning while he was on the pinnacle of power. He was arrested on 10th June, 1540, on a charge of `Treason, heresy, oppression, bribery, and extortion'. A Bill of Attainder was brought into Parliament on 19th June; instantly passed by acclamation, and Cromwell was beheaded on Tower Hill on 19th July. A speedy reversal of status and end of a life! Thus fell another favourite of Henry VIII - and St. Osyth Priory again reverted to the Crown.

Whether Cromwell was guilty of all the crimes alleged against him is hard to believe; but his arrogance, his pride and his acquisition of enormous estates aroused the enmity of the haughty nobles who despised him as a plebeian; while the poor of the land hated him for the subsidy he extracted from them. Marcus Brutus says in *Julius Caesar*,

Lowliness is young ambition's ladder,
Whereto the climber upward turns his face;
But when he once attains his utmost round,
He then unto the ladder turns his back,
Looks at the clouds, scorning the base degree
By which he did ascend.

Cromwell was an example of ambition that led to destruction, but perhaps his greatest error was to promote the marriage of the King with Anne of Cleves. When His Majesty became tired of her he turned upon those who had favoured her suit, and Cromwell's fate was sealed!

When Henry VIII got tired of a wife he served her as the Danes had done St Osyth, and straightaway married another. He sacked and burned monasteries and nunneries, sparing neither monk or nun; he defied the Pope, and destroyed anyone who openly objected to his own particular doctrines. A King who could do this was not likely to be very particular about the fate of his Ministers when they had served his purpose. Cromwell therefore, '... went up like a rocket and came down like a stick'. Perhaps it would have been better for him if he had remembered the fate of his master, Wolsey, who in the last extremity of his distress exclaimed:

> Had I but served my God with half the zeal
> I served my King, He would not in my age
> Have left me naked to my enemies

(King Henry VIII)

During the next three centuries the ownership of the estate passed through a number of hands until at last it was divided into several parts and sold piecemeal. One portion came into the possession of Richard Howard, who was born in 1692 and died in 1766; whose son was born in 1731. This son, William, married Elizabeth Brett and they had three daughters. At his death William bequeathed 'Bretts' and other property in St Osyth to his eldest daughter who had married Smith Bawtree. To Felicia, his second daughter, he left land in St Osyth and an estate in Clacton; and to his third daughter, Elizabeth, he gave 'Pilcroft Ironsides' and property in Clacton. It was upon these Clacton properties that the town of Clacton-on-Sea eventually arose.

A narrow winding road, more than a mile in length, connects the village of St Osyth with the beach of the same name. Here the modern contrast to ancient grandeur almost overwhelms the visitor. As far as the eye can see there are parked hundreds of caravans and mobile homes; row upon row, on both sides of the road; joining up with the holiday shackery which has spread from Jaywick. The foreshore is more or less in its natural state, undeveloped for several miles, the only outstanding object being the Martello Tower, a relic of the defences against Napoleon, and the huge concrete sea-wall, erected to repel the waves.

+++

Clacton-on-Sea, Frinton-on-Sea and Walton-on-the-Naze are three holiday centres which almost join each other as they stand on top of the cliffs which rise quite suddenly immediately north of Jaywick. These cliffs end equally abruptly at the Naze where, after a sharp dip to sea-level, the land becomes marsh again, surrounding Hamford Water.

The name for Clacton in *Domesday Book* is Clachintuna, which Morant thinks is derived from the Saxon words signifying `Clay' and `Tun', a `Town'. In Saxon times there were "i Villeins; XX bordars; XIII serfs; wood for CCCC swine; XX acres of meadow; i fishery; pasture for sheep; horse and beef beasts. It was worth XL pounds", and provided part of the revenue for the upkeep of the Bishopric of London.

At the time of the Conquest it was not separated into two parishes - `Great' and `Little' Clacton - a division which has been made since. `Little' is not much more than a group of houses lining a wide road which runs to the sea; but `Great Clacton' is a place of great antiquity, where Roman, Saxon and Norman burial places have been found. It preserves with pride thatched cottages of the 17th century, an inn of the Elizabethan era, a Norman doorway to the Church, a font over five hundred years old and rare vaulting to the roof of the nave. Students of ecclesiastical history will be interested to know that Eleazor Knox, the son of John Knox, the Puritan Divine of Geneva and Edinburgh, was Vicar here until his death in 1591.

There is another side to the Clacton of earlier days: Jaywick, (formerly `Jay-wic') was formerly part of the Manor, and at one time belonged to Captain Wegg, about whom there "...hangs a tale." The East Anglian coast was well known for the activities of organised, bold and ferocious gangs of smugglers. Any student of 18th century local history will have heard of Margaret Catchpole and her tragic lover; and of the Hadleigh and Sizewell Gangs;

Clacton on Sea

St Mary's, Frinton on Sea

about whom more will be told later in this narrative. Captain Wegg, a retired sea skipper, was said to be an active leader in their nefarious business, and to have made a fortune from the `trade', enough to buy what is now Jaywick and. build a substantial house with several acres of land.

Clacton-on-Sea, which sprang into strong and healthy existence, experienced such a rapid development that it is almost phenomenal. It is estimated that in the early years of the 19th century the population numbered 1,075; a hundred and fifty years later the town is one of the most popular and most visited holiday resorts.

The development of Clacton-on-Sea started in a very simple way when Mr Sargent Lay of Colchester was looking for a healthy spot in which to recuperate, and fixed his mind or a site on the cliff top between Great Clacton and Holland. The land was not then for sale, but in 1865 it was acquired, and, under the guiding hand of Peter S Bruff, Clacton-on-Sea arose. The modern town has little to attract the historian or the antiquarian; it is modern, and proud of it. Everything is designed to attract the holidaymaker; the famous pier, promenades and cliff walks make an attractive setting for holiday entertainment of every sort.

Frinton is a smaller parish, with the remains of the smallest church in the Tendring Hundred; but it has a long history.

In the time of Edward the Confessor it was called `Frientuna' or `Frietuna', a name probably derived from `Frie', a Saxon goddess, and `tun', a town. When the Norman Survey was undertaken the town belonged to Geoffrey de Mandeville, whose estates, mainly gifts from the Conqueror, stretched from the coast across country to Hertfordshire; a possession which he shared with Eustace, Earl of Bologne. In the reign of Henry II, the Manor was in the possession of the Tregoz family of Tolleshunt D'Arcy, who held it until the first rector, the Revd. Thomas Godmead, was appointed in 1321. During succeeding years it changed hands many times; in 1498 Phillippa Warner owned it, and in 1585 it was sold to Edward Grimston of Bradfield.

The Grimston family played an important part in the development of this area of Essex. They claimed descent from one, Sylvester, Standard Bearer to William the Conqueror at the Battle of Hastings, who took his name 'Grimston' from a place in Yorkshire which was given to him as his share in the Norman plunder. Sir Edward Grimston was Member of Parliament for Ipswich in the reign of Elizabeth I, and Controller of Calais in 1552. When the Duke of Guise captured Calais, Grimston was imprisoned in the Bastille, from which he escaped by exchanging clothes with his servant, filing through the bars of a window and lowering himself to the ground by a rope which his servant brought for him. This man was the father of Edward Grimston of Bradfield.

This Edward Grimston married a daughter of Thomas Risby of Lavenham, who was also a grand-daughter of John Harbottle of Crosfield. Their eldest son, Harbottle Grimston was created a Baronet in 1612, and was Sheriff of Essex in 1614. His son, Sir Harbottle, became an eminent lawyer, was Member of Parliament for Colchester and Speaker of the House of Commons. His son, Sir Samuel, died without male issue, when the Baronetcy became extinct. By his will the estate was left to his nephew, William Luckyn, on condition that he took the name of Grimston.

He did so, and was made Baron Dunboyne, 2nd Viscount Grimston, in 1719. He married a daughter of James Cook, citizen of London, and had nineteen children

In a reference to the Harbottles, Camden says, "Where the Coquet springs among the rough and stony mountains of Cheviot, is Harbottle; in the Saxon tongue '... the station of the army', whence the family of the Harbottles descended".

The heirs of Sir Harbottle Grimston sold Frinton to a Wapping mariner named Warren, in 1691, one of whose daughters married James Bushell, another mariner, and famous for 'Fishing for Wrecks'. Ownership subsequently passed through several hands, the last person to have total possession seems to have been George Lynne, towards the end of the 18th century.

Much of the original parish has disappeared because of erosion by the sea, but beautiful golden sands remain, from where the first under-water telephone cable was laid to a lighthouse at sea, on 2nd October, 1893. Today Frinton-on-Sea is sedate; the famous greensward between the road and the cliff-top being a unique feature of the town, calling to mind memories of uniformed nannies with their privileged charges. Day trippers are *infra dig*, beach parties are frowned upon, but the sea and the sands are open for everyone to enjoy.

Among the various tenures and manorial customs of ancient days there was one by which two or three parishes could be united and enrolled as one district under the Saxon liberty of Sac, Soc or Soken; in order that they might enjoy certain favours, privileges and exemptions. These Sokens bore a resemblance to Aldermanries or Baronial Jurisdictions; and descended from father to son. They gave the Lords of the Manor who owned them important and far-reaching powers, even of hanging culprits who had incautiously strayed into their legal preserves: a Right known by the Norse terms of *infangenetheof* and *utfangenetheof*.

Many Sokens belonged to Church dignitaries; Philip Morant mentions one in Colchester connected with St Mary's Church and owned by the Bishop of London. In William Stubb's *County History* it is said, "The right of Sac and Soc was terrible in the days of Stephen, but in ordinary times the Courts, exercising their jurisdiction according to the custom of the Manor, and not according to the Will of its Lord, soon became harmless enough."

In the Tendring Hundred the parishes of Thorpe, Kirby and Walton were united, "... *tria juncta in uno*"; and, in 941, were given by Athelstan, the English King, to the Church of Saint Paul, under the name of Eudulphesnesa or Alduluesnasa. `Eudulphes - nesa' obviously is derived from Eudulf, a known Saxon Thane; and `nesa' or `Nase' from a promontory or point of land jutting into the sea. This surely distinguishes one of the three parishes *in tria juncta*, which is now called Walton-on-the-Naze, or, more properly, Walton-le-Soken.

The Parish of Walton then consisted of the small peninsula, and Morant wrote of how "... the raging sea keeps daily undermining and encroaching upon this parish". Even then steps were taken to protect it with a primitive kind of sea wall, and the name of `Wall Town` was given to the area because of the embankment or wall thrown up to hold back the sea. The projecting point of land suggested the `Naze' or Nose.

When Claudius, the Roman Emperor, invaded England in AD 40 or 43, he brought with him, according to Dion Cassius, many elephants, the first to be seen in this country. With these he crossed the Thames from Kent into Essex, where he conquered the natives and established Roman settlements. In 1701 bones of an extraordinary size were found on the banks of the River Stour at Wrabness near Harwich. These may reasonably be supposed to be the bones of one of these enormous animals.

William Camden, the historian who published his *Britannia* in 1586, does not devote a great deal of space to Essex, but he does say "In King Richard's time, on the sea shore at a village called Eudulphnesse, were found two teeth of such bigness that two hundred such teeth as men have might have been cut out of them". Ralph, the Monk of Coggeshall, who wrote three hundred and fifty years before Camden said he "saw these teeth", and connects them with the elephants of Claudius, "...the bones of which beasts have been found".

The archæologist can find evidence at Walton of flint workings and of tool making in the Stone Age; and the geologist finds his hunt for fossils rewarding as he searches among the Red Clay beds.

Domesday Book records "iii salt works" among the trio of united parishes for then the people made their salt from sea-water; a practice which extended to many places around the Norfolk coast with a collecting point at Salthouse, and from which that village took its name.

The cliffs at the Naze were found to contain horizontal layers of argillaceous limestone, with veins of calcareous spar. Known as septaria this 'Stone from the sea' was quarried and transported to Harwich where the larger lumps were treated and rendered suitable for use in building, the remainder being ground up for cement. Dale, in his *History of Harwich* says that "...with this (septaria) the walls of the town were built", and there is abundant evidence that it was widely used.

The old church at Walton was in ruins when Morant wrote his history of Essex; it has now been under the sea for almost two centuries, taking with it two parcels of land which were originally let to tenants to provide an income for "... the poor of the Parish". The rents paid were £15 per annum for one lot and £4.10.0 for the other; but eventually the sea robbed the poor even of this! Another Walton estate, also now beneath the sea, belonged to the Prebends of St Paul's Church in London, associated with... "the thirteenth stall in the left side of the choir of the Cathedral".

But the sea, having devoured it all, the endowment is now marked *Probenda Consumpta per Mare*. As though the loss of these acres was not enough, a farm of fifty-six acres of freehold land, and another of thirty-four acres of copyhold, which the Governors of Queen Anne's Bounty bought for the augmentation of the Living of Holy Trinity, Colchester, have gone also.

In a book entitled *Sea Mirrour*, published in 1625, a Dutchman named Wilhelm Johnson Blaeuw advised mariners to look for a house on the Naze and use it as a 'Sea-mark'; seventy years later Captain Grenville Collins, who is described as Hydrographer in Ordinary to their most excellent Majesties King William III and Queen Mary, wrote another book, *Survey of the Sea Coast of England and Scotland*, in which he gave the most elaborate instructions to seamen to steer by the Naze "... which may be known by the trees and a house that standeth on it".

By the year 1719 the said 'House' was deteriorating and the trees rotting and falling down, so the Secretary of the Lords Commons of the Admiralty requested the Elder Brethren of Trinity House to erect "... a proper sea-mark... to the benefit of navigation". Investigations as to the suitability of a site, its availability and the cost of building eventuated in a decision to erect a Tower on the Naze. Work proceeded speedily, and on 1st November in the same year the *London Gazette* advertised the "... new sea-mark on the Cliffs of the Naze, a Tower eighty-one feet high which, standing on cliff, themselves one hundred and thirty eight feet high, would serve as a guide to mariners through the Gold Mere Gat and by Long Sand Head, Fifteen Miles out to sea". The Tower became almost an amenity of Walton, being described in the guide books as "... a place from whence one seeth a large prospect of the coasts of Essex and Suffolk; the town and port of Harwich; and Men of War riding at anchor at the Gun Fleet".

During the First World War the Tower was used by Observers who kept a look-out for German warships: during the Second it housed a Signals Wing. In 1942 it was involved in plotting the Action against the *Scharnhorst* and the *Gneisenau*, and in the next year it was attacked by six Focke-Wolfe 190s. There was some damage to the property and four people were killed, but the Signals Station survived. A second attack eleven weeks later resulted in damage to telephones and mains, but again the essential equipment was untouched. After that the Luftwaffe left the Tower alone. Today it stands desolate upon the Naze, the door nailed shut and bearing a notice threatening a fine of £50 for anyone causing damage to the property.

As a holiday resort Walton is different from either Clacton or Frinton: it is a Mecca for coach parties, which, while being discouraged at Frinton, are welcomed here with open arms. Walton is a lively resort; in its own individual way, with the air full of the accents of visitors from London's East End predominating.

+++

Where the cliffs of the Naze end abruptly the lower lands of 'Mose' begin, and the innumerable creeks and islands of Hamford Water. On comparatively higher ground, overlooking the Sokens and far away to sea, stands Beaumont or, as its name implies, 'the fine hill'. It may be a small parish, but it has a distinctive history.

In olden times there were two small and dilapidated churches, that of Beaumont, overshadowed by the great manorial Hall, was set among mighty trees and dedicated to Saint Leonard; that of Moze stood in a hollow and was in such a ruinous state "...the steeple thereof having already fallen" that an Act of Parliament was obtained in 1678 to unite the two parishes and use only one church building. What was left of Moze church was demolished, the materials being salvaged to repair the Beaumont Church. Tithes and emoluments belonging to Moze were directed to Beaumont, and the union of Beaumont with Moze was complete.

It is strange that of the two parishes Beaumont should be that to survive, because there is no mention of it in Domesday or in any old authority, until 1242; whereas Moze, with Saxon Manorial status, was of the greater importance, to which Beaumont appears to have been an appendage.

Soon after the accession of Richard II in 1377, village people began to rebel against the Feudal Laws, the exaction of the nobility from their retainers, and the heavy taxes imposed. Men like Watt Tyler, John Ball and Jack Straw fomented insurrections, and a rising took place which threatened to overthrow the Constitution. Breaking out in this otherwise quiet corner of Essex, the insurrection continued more or less throughout the turbulent reign of King Richard whose great favourite was Robert de Vere, then the owner of the Manor of Beaumont.

Robert de Vere was a young man "...of good figure and insinuating address", but of dissolute morals; and, by fostering and aiding the vices of the King, he acquired great influence over him, causing de Vere to become the most detested person in the Realm. His ambitions culminated in his amassing such power that, like Thomas Cromwell in after times, he became the envy and detestation of both nobles and people; only avoiding the execution block by escaping to the Continent, when all his possessions, including Beaumont, were confiscated to the Crown.

In 1389 the king granted Beaumont to Joane de Bohun, Countess of Essex; but the de Veres, in the person of Alberic, 10th

Earl of Oxford, obtained a restoration of the estate. When Richard Plantagenet, Duke of Gloucester, became, by devious ways, King Richard III, he gave the Manor of Beaumont to John Howard, Duke of Norfolk. In 1483 the Duke was killed at the side of Richard at the Battle of Bosworth, and Henry Tydder, who succeeded to the throne as Henry VII, gave Beaumont back to the de Veres. The lands and other assets of the parish eventually passed into the hands of the Darceys of Saint Osyth; on to the Earl of Guildford, who was Patron of the Living until 1743, and then to Guy's Hospital.

Whatever the calibre of these men of old may have been, there was none of them so great as a modern hero, who sleeps within the shadow of this village church. Lord [Julian] Byng, who died in 1935, was one of the heroes of our time, who led the Canadian Forces in the Great War, achieving such fame that his name will be for ever associated with Vimy Ridge. In the post-war years he distinguished himself as Governor-General of Canada and Chief Commissioner of the Metropolitan Police.

+++

The two parishes, Great and Little Oakley, are described in Domesday as 'Accleia', belonging, at least in part, to Robert Geronis (or Gernon) of Stansted Montfichet. The name 'Oakley' is derived from 'Ac' (the Saxon for 'Oak') and 'Ley' (a pasture). Apart from the recital of the names of the various claimants to the Manorial Rights, there is nothing much to say about them, until examination of the Parish Registers reveals some most interesting entries. The earliest date of these journals is 1558, the first year of the reign of Elizabeth I, and the first entry for Little Oakley reads:

"OKELEY PARVA - 1598 - 9v. 1558.

> The register, or booke, of recorde, contayning the names of all such as have been baptized, married or buried, from ye first yeare of the reign of our Soverigne Lady Elizabeth, by the Grace of God of England, Ffrance, and Ireland Queen, Defender of the Faith.

Being the yeare after the creation of the world, ffyve thousand ffyve hundred twenty-ffyve, and the yeare since the Sonne of God took fleshe of the Virgin and became man, a thousand fyve hundred and fiftie-eight." [Note the different spellings of the word `Five'.]

The ancient historian placed both 1598 and 1558 at the head of his records, but the dates with subsequent entries make it clear that 1558 is correct. He is also somewhat incorrect as to the age of the world, but it is nevertheless curious as a calculation of his time.

The first entry of a christening in the Register is:

"Imprimis. Goodlie Weld, the daughter of John Weld, was christened the first of Anno Sepradicto."

The first entry in the list of marriages reads:

"qy. 1558. It., that Richard Dood, the labourer, was married to Anne Smile, the xvth March".

In the reign of Charles II, England's woollen industry was thought to be in decline and in order to stimulate the use and sale of woollen materials an Act of Parliament was passed compelling the burying of corpses in woollen shrouds or coverings. It was incumbent upon the officiating Clergy that they should have a formal certificate that the corpse was so clothed before they continued with the Burial Service. In the Little Oakley Register there is this entry :

"Burials anno 1733. Abraham Makings, Susan Harris, affidavits that ye persons whose names are here inserted were buried in nothing but was made of sheep's wool, were made according to Act of Parliament, and delivered to me, T. Gibson, Curate".

This Act was repealed under George III.

To show that civil marriage is not an invention of the 20th century, but was common three hundred years earlier, there is this entry:

"1654. William Palmer, single man, and Sarah Bridge ye daughter of Thomas Bridge, Alderman of Harwich, deceased, and now ye daughter-in-law of John Malden, Minister of ye Parish were married before Mr. Rutland, Justice of ye Peace of ye towne of Colchester, upon the 21st day of September, 1654".

Collections for Charitable purposes were even then not unknown:

"Collected for ye towne of Pontefract, in Yorkshire, For the re-building of the Parish Church, being destroyed in the warre, 1s. 9d."

+++

The influence of the port and parish of Harwich would seem to predominate over Dovercourt, but as the latter was the 'Mother' Parish it must be considered first.

The name is derived from 'Dwfr', 'Dubro' or 'Duvrisc', all meaning a 'race or tide of water'; and 'Cwrr', 'a border or edge'. It is an ancient parish which rose into prominence halfway through the 19th century when an enterprising gentleman, then the local Member of Parliament, launched it as a seaside resort. An undercliff walk, over a mile in length was built along the sea-shore in 1858 and, to this day, remains the best feature of the town. The old part of the village, now designated 'Upper Dovercourt', has the Parish Church on the main road to Ramsey and Colchester. There was formerly a Guild or Fraternity of Saint George in connection with this Church, and the George Inn, on the opposite side of the road, had connections with this organisation.

In John Foxe's *Book of Martyrs* there is the story of Dovercourt's once famous Rood, which was credited with such sanctity that miraculous powers were attributed to it; so much so that votaries and pilgrims with their offerings were attracted in great numbers. It was believed, for example, that its powers were such that no man could close the door of the Church upon it, and that anyone attempting to do so would suffer instant death: the doors of the Church, therefore, were left open day and night. There were, however, those who did not so believe, holding such theories to be superstitions and idolatrous practices, and one night in 1532 four men ruthlessly tore the Rood from its fastenings and burnt it to ashes on the Green outside the Church. For this act described as "... felony and sacrilege" Robert King and Robert Debenham of East Bergholt and Nicholas Marsh of Dedham were convicted and hanged in chains, while the fourth man, Robert Gardiner, also of Dedham, escaped.

Like Beaumont, Dovercourt is the resting place of one of the heroes of the Great War, Charles A Fryatt. In August, 1914, when the Great War broke out, he was 42, and Captain of the Great Eastern Railway steamer *Brussels*, steaming regularly between England and Holland. After the Declaration of War, knowing that the Approaches and the Seaways were heavily mined, he continued his journeying, risking both mines and enemy submarines.

In March, 1915, he escaped an attack by a submarine and three weeks later, when he was attacked again, he retaliated by steaming straight at his enemy and ramming him. The following year Fryatt's ship was captured by two German destroyers and Fryatt himself taken prisoner. At a courtmartial the Captain's Log was produced in evidence against him and it was said that, although wearing uniform, he had no status as a combatant therefore his conduct was unlawful. The Bruges Court condemned him, and he suffered execution by shooting.

The indignation which was aroused in England and among her allies lasted until after the end of the war, then the Germans, while holding that the verdict was just, said that they regretted the haste with which the sentence had been carried out. In July, 1919, the body of Captain Fryatt was brought back to England and laid to rest at Dovercourt. The Fryatt Memorial Hospital stands as a monument to his memory.

+++

There would have been no Harwich if there had not been a town of Orwell, which once, it was said, stood upon rocks about five miles out to sea, and upon whose disappearance the town of Harwich arose. This legendary town, like so many others destroyed by the ever-changing pattern of the North Sea coasts, was submerged by the waters and now lies under the waves. That it had once been an important seaport can be gauged by a reference to it in the Prologue to the *Canterbury Tales* by Geoffrey Chaucer, where the Merchant wants the sea protected from Pirates "... betwixt Middlesburgh and Orwelle".

Chaucer became a member of the Royal Household in 1367 when he was described as a `Valletus' and an `esquier'. In time he became a member of the diplomatic corps, a justice of the peace, a member of Parliament, the clerk in charge of the king's building works and a forest official. The appointment which had direct connection with Orwell was that of Controller of Customs.

In 1374 Edward III appointed Chaucer `Controller of the export tax', or Customs Officer concerning wool, sheepskins and leather shipped through the Port of London. Wool was then England's principle export, and the taxes thus collected helped to finance Edward's wars in the 1340s and 1350s, together with his smaller military expeditions of the 1370s and 1380s. They also helped to pay for the extravagances of the Court of the King and, later, of his grandson, Richard II.

In 1382 Chaucer's responsibilities were extended to include controllership of customs on wine and other merchandise not covered by the Wool Tax. In such a position he would have an extensive knowledge of this country's export trade and of the ports through which it was handled, and thus be able to stress the importance of Orwell. Many places and references to events which he quotes in his works are based upon the experiences in his life, and Orwell is no exception, as it was the seaport of his native town of Ipswich.

Ancient charts and maps designate what is now known as `Harwich Harbour' as `Orwell Haven'; a shelter which has always been of great importance. Where the two Rivers, Stour and Orwell, meet and flow out to sea together they have created, through the centuries, a huge area of almost land-locked water. With the establishment and growth of the town of Harwich on its southern shore, and recently the developing modern Felixstowe on the north, the importance of Orwell Haven has been known to seafaring men ever since the first of them went "down to the sea in ships, that do business in great waters". Michael Drayton, referring to the confluence of the two rivers and the haven which their union created, wrote:

> Beside all the roads and havens in the east
> The harbour where they meet is reckoned best.

The destruction of the town of Orwell by the encroachment of the sea emphasises one of the peculiarities as well as the misfortunes of the East Coast of England. There can be no doubt that ever since the ocean originally broke in to separate the British Isles from the Continent, alterations in the size and shape of England have been going on. Much of the eastern side of the country that is now cultivated land, in particular the Fenlands, which were drained by Vermuyden and others, were formerly under water; and where now the tide regularly ebbs and flows was dry land. From Walton and Harwich to as far inland as Hertfordshire and Cambridgeshire, marine shells and other striking examples of fossilised underwater life have been found. At one time the villages of Whaddon and Barrington in Cambridgeshire were active centres for a thriving industry of coprolite digging. The existence of and the extraction of these petrified saurians from the solid chalk was conclusive proof that they would not have been there had not the area been covered by the sea at some time.

The Saxon King Alfrea, more popularly known as Alfred the Great, was twenty-three years old when he ascended the throne. During the years of his reign he fought nine battles with the marauding Danes, the most important being a victory over their seaborne forces at the mouth of the River Stour in the year 885. His victory was partly due to the fact that he had Orwell Haven in which to assemble and maintain his fleet. The Haven has been advantageous to naval, as well as commercial, activities ever since.

The name 'Harwich' or 'Herewic', as it was called in the early days, is derived from 'Pene-Pic', meaning '... a haven where an army lies' or 'an army's castle', and it would seem that, although Alfred won the battle, he did not win the war, but was forced to

Harwich; the Wheel Crane and the fishing port

keep an army at the site to oppose the piratical intruders. The account of the battle of 885 is one of the first recorded references to Harwich, but there was obviously occupation of the site in earlier years. The `Count of the Saxon Shore' maintained a military position there, coins from the Roman mint have been dug up, a tessellated pavement discovered, and a wall which was demolished in modern times was found to be constructed with Roman materials.

There is no mention of Harwich in Doomsday, which is not surprising, as at the time of the compilation of that survey, Harwich had no identity of its own, being merely an appendage of Dovercourt. By the 12th century, however, the town was growing into a unit in its own right, and was enclosed in a wall largely composed of Septaria, in which there were four gates: Water Gate, St Austin's Gate, St Helen's Port, and Castle Gate. It was made a Borough Corporate by a Charter of Edward II in 1318 and its privileges were increased by later grants.

The first Mayor of Harwich was John Hankin, elected to that Office in 1603, and the first Members of Parliament, of which the town had two, were John Butt and Thomas de Eaton, both elected in 1344. The Parish Church, founded by Roger Bigod, Earl of Norfolk, was originally a `Chapel of Ease' to the Mother Church at Dovercourt.

Harwich has a long and honourable naval tradition. Edward III set out from here in 1338 on his first expedition against France. It was active when the warning came of the approach of the Armada, and its sea-captains gained fame in the engagements which followed. Charles II knew the port well during the wars against the Dutch, while in the Parish Church hang the flags which billowed to the breeze from the boats of the Harwich Flotilla during the war of 1914-1918. Since the days when men from Harwich sailed with Sir Francis Drake there have been few braver deeds at sea than those of the men of the Harwich minesweepers, who held the record of enemy mines swept up from the sea-ways in any theatre of war.

The Navy-yard Wharf at Harwich, originally the Navy Yard, is the site of the Ship Yard which Queen Elizabeth came to inspect in 1561. Ship building was developed there, particularly when Samuel Pepys was Member of Parliament for Harwich and, as a member of the Government, Secretary for the Navy. Deane, the ship builder, and Pepys were personal friends, as well as both being Members of Parliament for the Borough. Need one say more?

The old bell hanging by the entrance gates to the Yard was cast by John Darby, bellfounder of Ipswich in 1666. Housed originally in a Bell Tower, where it was rung daily to summon men to work. Disposed of in 1920, it was recovered in 1930 and re-hung in its present position.

In the Church Register, which begins in the second year of the reign of Elizabeth I, is the record of the birth of Christopher Newport, a seaman who shared in Sir Walter Raleigh's settlement of Virginia; and the same Register has entries recording the two marriages of Christopher Jones, the Master of the *Mayflower*, which sailed out of Harwich on the memorable voyage.

There are a number of other sites in Harwich also of outstanding historical interest.

The Redoubt (a word which *Nuttall's Standard Dictionary* defines as meaning "... a temporary fort usually without flanking defences") formed part of the Martello Tower chain of defences extending from Aldeburgh to Seaford, and was one of four such constructions, the others being at Dungeness, Hythe, and Eastbourne. Built in 1808 on a hill which was crowned with an elm tree so conspicuous that it was marked on old charts as a landmark for mariners, the work caused the `London Road' to be diverted to its present `Main Road' position. The fort was positioned on the top of the hill with a retaining wall around it, the area between the dry wall and the fort buildings forming a dry moat of some considerable depth. Soil, with which to form supporting `earth-works', was transported by pannier donkeys from a low-lying part of the town known as Bathside. This excavation had serious repercussions many years after: in 1953 the East Coast Floods rushed into this area, which was below sea-level, destroying property and claiming eight lives.

Lighthouses were introduced at Harwich at a very early stage in the development of the town. The first, and somewhat primitive attempt at aiding navigation by means of a light on shore was by burning six candles, each weighing one pound, in a room with a glazed front situated at the southern extremity of the town; so placed to warn approaching vessels of a sand-bank stretching across the entrance to the harbour.

In the time of Charles II this purpose was served more efficiently by two wooden light-houses erected on the shore. These were re-built with stone in 1818, and the owner, General Rebow, made a fortune by charging one penny per ton 'Light Dues' on all cargo coming into the port. Acquired by Trinity House in 1836, they subsequently became redundant because of the changing course of the channel.

Known as the 'High and Low Lighthouses', the taller is a ninety feet high, nine sided tower, built of grey gault brick; and the Low Light, built of brick, is ten sided, standing forty-five feet in height. They stand 150 yards apart, and worked as a pair, so that when seen from the sea, one light was correctly positioned exactly above the other, the vessel knew that it was on the right course. In 1909 they were sold to Harwich Borough Council; the High Light became a residence and the Low Light reverted to Trinity House to become a Pilot signal station.

One antique of exceptional interest, standing on the Green near the lighthouses, is the Tread-wheel Crane. Built in 1667 on the site of the old Naval Yard, this machine is the only British example of its kind still in existence. It was moved to its present site in 1932. The crane was worked by male prisoners from the local gaol, prisoners of war or paupers walking INSIDE the great wheels. The only form of a brake was a spar which, when necessary, was thrust against the outer edge of one of the wheels. It does not require much imagination to think of what might, indeed did happen when the tread-wheel flew back. Should the load outbalance the power the men inside the wheel would be revolved backwards, with disastrous results.

Halfpenny Pier is so called because of the half-penny toll charged in earlier days for pedestrian entrance. The popular paddle steamers which, until the 1930s, plied between Harwich, Felixstowe and Ipswich, departed from this pier, from which today the ferry to Felixstowe operates.

In the area of water enclosed by the arm of the pier, a space called The Pond, the Royal National Lifeboat Institution lifeboat is moored, as are also the Pilot Launches with which Pilots go out to meet ships at sea in order to navigate them into the harbour.

Harwich has an important commercial history, fluctuating through the years in both volume and profitability.

Preparations for the sailing of the fleet of Edward III brought a good deal of trade to the town, an example of more than one aspect of its naval importance. Commercial usage was established in the 14th century when it had become the principal East Coast port for the exporting of cloth to the Continent. Within a hundred years the traders of Harwich were importing wine; beginning to trade with Russia; and local fishermen were setting their sails toward the Icelandic fishing grounds.

Many of the houses in the town's chief thoroughfares were re-fronted in Georgian times, a period of outstanding prosperity for the local community. Too many questions should not be asked as to the source of this prosperity or the wealth which accrued to many of the townsfolk: but conclusions may be drawn from the fact that the cellars of the majority of the houses were inter-communicating for the double purpose of the speedy disposal of smuggled goods when the 'Preventive Men' (Customs Officials) were on patrol; and also to provide a way of escape from the Press Gangs.

The fortunes of Harwich waxed in times of war, and waned in times of peace, a fact which had an influence upon the way in which property was either preserved or neglected. During the latter half of the 19th century, the first half of the 20th, and because of the ravages of the World Wars, neglect and decay wrought havoc in most parts of the town; but there is still much to be seen to remind one of the glories of the past, while the restorations taking place in modern times are doing much to make Harwich attractive once more.

+++

Into Harwich Harbour flow the rivers Orwell (which begins life as the Gipping) and Stour, and attention must be paid to the latter because of its geographical importance.

Physically the Stour is as unlike the Orwell as could be, being broad and shallow with a number of muddy bays, such as Seafield Bay, Jacques Bay and Cooperus Bay. Arthur Young, the 18th century writer and agriculturist, who considered the river to be "... singularly pleasing" was wise enough to advise that it should be viewed "... when the tide is in."

It must have been considered an important river in the days of the early settlements in the Eastern Counties because it was chosen to serve as a frontier between the East Saxon and the Anglian Kingdoms; as commemorated by Edmund Spenser, when he wrote:

> The Stour, that parteth with his pleasant floods
> The Eastern Saxons from the Southern Nye,
> And Clare and Harwich both doth beautify.

+++

The River Stour is tidal up as far as Manningtree, and was navigable for vessels of up to one hundred tons, a fact which contributed much to the former prosperity of the town.

In the Middle Ages it was a place of considerable importance. In the early years of that era the main means of both internal and external trade was through Markets or Fairs. The right to grant these was the feudal prerogative of the overlord of the town, usually the King; and when the town bought their freedom from their overlord they normally obtained Charters to hold these events.

Markets were local affairs, to satisfy the needs of the neighbourhood; fairs, on the other hand, were international, enabling merchants from all over Europe to meet and do business. To these great events came merchants from Flanders and Germany wines, shearers with the wool-clips from Wales, shippers with French wines and clothiers with the finished goods, gowns, jerkins and hose; so the town fashions came to the country. In search of these things flocked all the gentry of the shire, and of neighbouring shires too, lordlings, knights, yeomen, with their wives and daughters. Goods for their own subsistence they grew, bred, brewed, spun or wove for themselves, but once a year they came to buy the luxuries, cloth, wines and rare preserved fruits; all the treasures that appeared on the first day and had vanished when the fair ended.

It was usual for a Fair to coincide with the Festival or Feast Day of the local Church and to continue for up to ten days; thus not only was the sanctity of the church added to what was termed 'The Peace of the Fair', but it was ensured that the largest number of people would be present.

These gatherings attracted the 'Strolling Players' or 'Mummers'; who enacted curious old plays called Moralities, in which characters bore such names as Iniquity, Vanity, and Vice. Another form of entertainment at the Manningtree Fair was the roasting of a whole ox with a stuffing of a pudding-like substance; a practice to which Shakespeare alludes in *Henry IV*, when Prince Hal, among many opprobrious names calls the truculent Falstaff "... a Manningtree ox with a pudding in his belly".

In their report to Edward VI the Royal Commissioners speak of Manningtree as "... a great Towne, and also a haven Towne, having in yt to the number of seven-hundred houseling people". It may seem to be remarkable today to regard a place with seven hundred inhabitants as '... a great Towne', but in the period under review there were no great industrial centres, and the entire population of England numbered less than five million people.

Manningtree Parish Church of St Michael was originally built in the 13th century, re-built in the year in which Shakespeare died, re-fronted in 1886, restored in 1901 and finally demolished because of dry rot in 1967. Formerly it was a Chapel of Ease to the original Mistley Church, the remains of which stand on Mistley Heath. That was the first of the three Churches of Mistley, the second was the Adam church built on the bank of the River, of which the famous Towers still remain. The third, the present church, St Mary's, was built in New Road in 1865. It is ironic that with the demolition of St Michael's, which was constituted a Parish in its own right at the beginning of the 19th century, its congregation has to revert to the church at Mistley from where the ecclesiastical benefice began.

Archbishop William Laud was greatly interested in Manningtree church and among its most treasured possessions was a Communion Set presented by him and bearing his Arms. In the Church was a Memorial Tablet in memory of the celebrated Thomas Tusser, `the Father of English agriculture' and author of *Five hundred points of good husbandry*. Another tablet, set up in 1748, told how, on the green at the top of the hill, Thomas Osmond, a cloth worker, was burned to death for his faith, under the orders of the renowned Bishop Edmund Bonner, in 1555

One other greatly prized possession of Manningtree Church was one of only three religious paintings by John Constable. The subject was The Ascension; and when the Church was demolished the painting was given to Feering, in which church it found a new home. The other two Constable paintings of a religious character are at Nayland and Brantham.

To mention Manningtree is recall Matthew Hopkins. The son of a Suffolk minister and trained in the law, Hopkins set himself out to be a Witch-finder in the days when the popular mind was prone to great excitement and fear of witches. By exploiting the fears of the people Hopkins enriched himself, and sent so many people to their doom that eventually clergy and laity alike were so antagonised that the Finder himself was apprehended, tried and condemned as he had condemned many others. In contrast to

Hopkins, another native of Manningtree was John Watson. He entered the ministry of the church and, under the *nom-de-plume* of Ian McLaren wrote that wonderful book *Beside the bonnie briar bush* and other works.

There is a somewhat lengthy rhyme describing Manningtree as it was in the middle of the 18th century. Entitled *Reminiscences of Manningtree*, it was composed by Joseph Glass and published in 1885 by J H Woodley, 30 Fore Street, City of London. Running to 344 lines, it gives a comprehensive account of the town and its activities, as viewed from various angles. It begins:

> It is a pleasant market town,
> As broad as long, of some renown;
> And from the river's side 'tis seen
> Mid rising ground of verdant green.
> Its ancient name was Schidingchou,
> Centuries have passed since then, and now;
> And by its aborigines
> 'Twas noted for its many trees.

It then refers to people and events which have already been mentioned in this text: the burning of the Dovercourt Rood, and how one of the condemned was hanged at Manningtree;

> And one of the outrageous three
> Was hung in chains at Manningtree.

Thomas Osmond's martyrdom; and Matthew Hopkins: and then goes on, in a slightly humorous vein, to speak of two more who were certainly characters in their day:

> One rainy day at Manningtree,
> Twas in the Eighteenth Century,
> One Sunday morning, just at Ten
> That Madam Burton, there and then
> With her umbrella passed along
> To Church, with an admiring throng.
> She held it high above her head,
> The first that had been seen, 'twas said:
> Some knowing townsfolk were agreed

Manningtree a century and a half ago

It was a most presumptuous deed;
That pride induced an act so vain
And not a shelter from the rain
As was alleged, but ostentation
And should be held in detestation
They thought that some of higher birth
Would soon disdain to tread the earth;
Were thankful that themselves were saved
From being proud, and thus depraved.
Then there was Mr Spink:
The saddle-maker, Mr Spink,
About this time was led to think
That sermons, generally, if understood
By listening hearers, might do good;
But most decidedly he thought it wrong
That ministers should ever make them long,
For then 'twas clear, they over-stepped the line
When people had arranged the time to dine,
The Pastor should, he said, dismiss his flock
Precisely at the hour of Twelve o'Clock;
If not, just as he heard the Church-bell strike;
Although in some respects he did not like
He would not hesitate, or longer stay
But take his hat and stick, and walk away
Declaring that his dinner he preferred
To any sermon that he ever heard.

After this the rhyme goes on to describe houses, buildings, roads, clubs, churches and schools; altogether a descriptive account of the life of in Manningtree in those days.

In the reign of Richard II Manningtree appeared in public records as a small ship-building centre; an industry which did not develop; probably because of its shallow water-front; but it did become a busy trading port, chiefly as a transit location for Dedham and Sudbury during the prosperous days of the woollen Industry in East Anglia. The importance of the Stour at that time may be gauged by some old charts naming it Manningtree Water. In the 16th century enterprising local merchants took part in sending boats to the Icelandic fishing grounds; prompting Norden in 1594 to describe Manningtree as "... a little fisher town".

At the time of the Dissolution of the Monasteries Manningtree was assessed for Hearth Tax and the Returns of 1662 show the town was known to have 211 Hearths, with neighbouring Mistley having 60.

By the end of the 17th century the Stour had, in parts, become almost choked with growing weeds, and in 1705 the Corporation of Sudbury obtained an Act of Parliament granting them power to open up the river as far as Manningtree; and for many years after it became a highway to the sea for bricks, chalk and lime, with the boats carrying coal on the return journey. Cargoes were carried in lighter barges, twenty-seven feet long, with a capacity of twenty-six tons: these were drawn by horses, as depicted in a number of Constable's paintings. At Manningtree trans-shipment to larger craft took place. Steam driven barges first plied on this stretch of the river in 1864, and continued until the company which operated them went into liquidation in 1933; by which time the Sudbury merchants had found that it was much quicker to transport their merchandise by road.

+++

In mediæval days Mistley was "... faded and obscure" in relation to Manningtree; and so it continued until, in the early 18th century, Richard Rigby inherited Mistley Hall and its estates, and set about developing the whole area, with the object of creating a Port and Spa.

Rigby engaged Robert Adam, the leading architect of the day, to design the proposed development with shipyards, quays, warehouses and maltings on the one side and all the amenities of a fashionable Watering Place nearby; such as a Bathing Pavilion, fountains, a new Church, and an inn with `... Neat houses' and a village Green. When completed it would have been a charming place, but the dream was never fulfilled.

54

Richard Rigby died in 1788, leaving no heir and in 1844 the land earmarked for the Town and Port was divided into forty-five lots and sold by auction. Adam's ideas of a new Mistley were allowed to decay, but while little now remains of his planning, there is still an aura about the place which marks it as somehow 'different' because of an association which cannot be specified. As already noted, the twin towers of Adam's classical church stand beside the river; the corniced front of what was to have been the 'Spa Pavilion' with a Swan fountain in a round basin standing before it remains; and Georgian houses on the Green survive as relics of the grand design.

More could be said about the Stour: questions arise for which answers cannot be found. What history remains in the Creeks which have such curious names; Ballister, Gallister and Shallager? Where was Whitlowness? Was it a place where ship-levies were collected? Shall we ever know; does it really matter? All the sailor who drops anchor off Wrabness wants is a good anchorage and a friendly pub ashore.

Turn of this century Mistley

55

SUFFOLK

It is difficult to understand why East Anglia has failed to capitalise on one of the great human dramas which was enacted in its midst. The Stour Valley has John Constable, whose name is associated with the area around Dedham and East Bergholt; known far and wide as 'Constable Country', it draws thousands of visitors every year. Somerset has Lorna Doone; Yorkshire is promoting what it calls 'Herriot Country', based upon stories and films; yet here in Suffolk there is a real life historical drama, authenticated by a clergyman, but doing nothing about it! What Lorna Doone is to Oare, Margaret Catchpole should be to the East Anglian coastline about Felixstowe.

Margaret Catchpole was notorious - yet nobody ever hears about her. In Somerset, Blackmore's great story is exploited everywhere in the Doone Valley, by Bagworthy Water, and at Oare Church, where it is said she was married to John Rigg and where one is shown the window through which the shot was fired which spilled her blood upon the altar steps. Anywhere between Glastonbury and Land's End one can hear the story of Lorna Doone, but ask any ordinary person in Suffolk about Margaret Catchpole, and they will respond with a stare and an indecisive 'don't know'.

But they should know! What Blackmore did for Somerset, Cobbold has done for Suffolk, and if that part of the county were deservedly named 'Catchpole Country' and popularised as it should be, it could become a centre for interesting tourism as well as any other. Here is an epic of rural England; a true portrayal of the days of smuggling, an activity as rampant on England's East Coast as it was on the west.

Margaret Catchpole was born in 1773, the youngest of a labourer's six children. At an early age she showed her love for, and a masterly way with, horses; a characteristic which was to have such an influence upon her life. As a girl of thirteen, riding her horse bare-backed, she galloped the nine miles to Ipswich to fetch a doctor to a woman in urgent need of medical attention, for which action the girl was universally commended. In common with the majority of girls from her social background, Margaret entered into domestic service and found employment in the house of John Cobbold, the Ipswich brewer (whose firm still survives).

Romance entered her life in the person of Will Laud, a boatman of Felixstowe, who, in addition to his legitimate calling, was also a member of one of the fiercest gangs of smugglers on the East Coast. After one encounter with the 'Preventive Men' (the Customs and Excise Officers) his gang was so sought after by a combined Military and Police force, that they decided to run for it and scattered. Will Laud went to London, in hiding, but so distraught did Margaret become through fearing for his safety that, disguising herself as a sailor, she stole her master's horse and rode the seventy-odd miles to London to search for him.

Horse stealing was, according to the law of the land at that time, punishable by death, and, after her capture and due trial, this sentence was passed upon her. She escaped from Ipswich Prison (whether with the assistance of a sympathiser or not is unknown, or at least unstated), but was re-arrested and sentenced to the same punishment a second time. This was eventually commuted to transportation, and she was sent to Australia. Released after many years, she returned to Suffolk, where she died in 1841.

The Reverend Richard Cobbold, Rector of Wortham and Rural Dean, of the family by whom she had been formerly employed, wrote and published her life story, *The History of Margaret Catchpole; a Suffolk Girl*.

Unlike Blackmore's story of *Lorna Doone*, in which the action takes place in one valley and, although it may be 'based on fact', is largely apocryphal, the story of Margaret Catchpole is true, and involves many places spread over quite a wide area. Their identities are not disguised in the telling and on visiting them, even today, one can still feel the 'atmosphere' of days gone by.

This, then, is 'Catchpole Country':

NACTON; where Margaret lived in a cottage on a farm

where her father was employed.

FELIXSTOWE FERRY; the home of the girl's lover; Will Laud, who was apprenticed to a boat-builder at Aldeburgh and was the son of Stephen Laud, who plied the ferry boat between Felixstowe and Harwich. Their cottage stood in the shadow of a Martello Tower, where a huddle of old and odd buildings had become the dwelling places of men who lived their lives according to the dictates of their own desires, oblivious of the great world around and beyond them. It is easy to see why such a situation was a haven for smugglers.

BAWDSEY; where the smuggling fraternity had their 'headquarters'. From there they organised runs, landings, dispersals and hidings, all of which took a great deal of concentrated timing and briefing, not to mention arrangements for porterage and transport.

HOLLESLEY BAY was a well-known landing ground, with an environment so suitable for maritime activities that it was chosen at one time by Lord Nelson as a place in which to shelter his fleet. For the same reason it was a place where it was anticipated that Napoleon would attempt to invade.

The antiquity of the Abbey ruins at Butley, and the mediæval church at Shottisham were all turned to good account as hiding places for their contraband by the local people; while the oval tower of Ramsholt Church was used to show signals and guiding lights to the incoming boats from the sea.

'Catchpole Country' may be said to extend for the length of Hollesley Bay, as far north as Orford Ness, with the little town of that name nearby.

+++

Orford is a quiet place, at the tip of a peninsula between the River Ore and Butley. In mediæval times it was a thriving sea-port, one of those busy with the export of East Anglian woollen cloth, but the East Coast tides played the same trick on Orford as they did on other places by building up a bank of shingle across the harbour until approach to the choked-up shipping lanes was impossible. Today this shingle-bar extends for six miles, making a barrier inside which the River Ore curves until it reaches the sea at Shingle Street.

Orford is a town which has slowly died. A Subsidy-roll of 1327 suggests that the population at that time numbered about a thousand souls. The town prospered and was incorporated as a Free Borough in 1579, the first Mayor being James Coe, a merchant represented in brass in the church. A monastery of the Austin Friars was founded by Robert de Hewell in 1295, and during the following century two hospitals were built; that of St John the Baptist in 1320 and another dedicated to St Leonard, specifying that it was for lepers in 1390. By the 17th century decline in both population and trade was noticeable; in 1722 Daniel Defoe wrote; "... Orford was once a good town, but is decayed", a process which continued until disfranchisement took place in 1832; to be followed by dissolution fifty-four years later. Today the only signs of the little town's prosperous past are the curly gables of some of its houses, a sure sign of Dutch influence in their construction; the size and beauty of St Bartholomew's Church; and the great keep of Orford Castle.

'The ruined Castle, crumbling to decay'. (C. E. Benham)

Orford Castle is of most unusual shape, being polygonal on the outside and circular within. The outer walls and perimeter defences have long-since gone, but the Keep, with three square projecting towers, and a fore-building between the South Turret and the main structure, remain.

It was built by Henry II between 1166-1172 and has a romantic history. Hugh Bigod, Earl of Norfolk, who owned castles at Bungay, Framlingham and Thetford, attempted to take Orford, but was repulsed. Later it changed ownership on more than one occasion, notably when captured by the French invaders in 1217.

Originally the curtain enceinte had bastions, but no traces of the walls remain, the last section disintegrating in 1841. The keep was given to Robert Ufford, Earl of Suffolk, by Edward III in 1336, the building remaining in private ownership until 1962, when it was given to the Ministry of Public Buildings & Works.

The Crown & Castle Inn and the Castle, Orford

The Castle is mainly constructed of dressed Caen stone from Normandy, cemented with local septaria; and a deep well in the basement, with steps cut into the sides, is treated in the same way. The vaulting in the Chapel, and in the pointed windows, are among the earliest examples of Gothic architecture in England.

Entrance to the Castle is reached by a door at second-storey level; similar to that at Castle Hedingham. From a large entrance chamber a stone spiral stair-case leads to chambers previously occupied by Guards, apartments for a Priest, small rooms and a great circular room in which is a round table so large that it must have been constructed in the room it occupies. In the Norman Chapel there are ten round arches, slender pillars with carved capitals and a piscina and ambry by the Altar.

Concerning the well in the basement: the story goes that some Orford fishermen netted a `MerMAN' (not a `MerMAID' be it noted) and imprisoned this naked, wild and hairy creature (now portrayed on a sign-board in the street) in the Castle Well from which he somehow escaped and presumably returned to the sea.

Orford Ness was one of the most active areas for smuggling in the Margaret Catchpole saga, and for decades this century was surrounded by secrecy; the public being forbidden entrance for many years. It was there that Sir Robert Watson-Watt carried out his early experimental work on Radar, which was later transferred to Bawdsey further along the coast: the Ness became the property of the National Trust in 1993.

The nearby town of Ipswich figured largely in the Catchpole narrative, being the centre of both trade and law for the county, while the Butt and Oyster Inn at Chelmondiston on the lower reaches of the River Orwell was a much-frequented gathering place for the smuggling fraternity.

The author of *The History of Margaret Catchpole* described the district in which the events he recorded took place, when he wrote in 1847, as `... A large tract of extra-parochial land... known as Wolfkettle; the site of the famous Battle of Arwell, fought between the Earl of Ulfketel and the Danes in A.D. 1010. It was a wild waste, fit only for sheepwalks or a warren, or as a preserve for game'. He also writes in the Preface; `The public may depend upon the truth of the narrative. The author is the son of the lady with whom this extraordinary female (Margaret Catchpole) lived: and from whom he received the facts here given.'

It is interesting to ponder the likeness of `Wolfkettle' and `Ulfketel' and to notice their similarity to `Beowolf',`Wuffing' and `Offa', the latter often being written as `Uffa'.

THE SMUGGLERS OF THE
EAST ANGLIAN COAST

Some of the stories that have been written about smugglers have presented them in a semi-heroic light; but they were, after all, law-breakers, some were villains and even murderers; being just as bold and at times as ferocious as their counterparts, the wreckers in Cornwall. They were in line with the highwaymen; out to defeat the law in the search for personal gain. The true heroes of the time were the Officers of the Customs and Excise Department and the detachments of Dragoons who supported them.

The 18th and 19th centuries were times when very little respect was paid to the Excise Laws; most of the inhabitants of villages on or near the coast being concerned, in one way or another, with smuggling ventures. Nor did this apply to the working class of the population only: farmers and squires formed Joint Stock Companies, holding shares of £10 or £20 each in order to finance the operations of the smugglers so that goods could be purchased in the Low Countries, shipped, and landed on the East Anglian coast.

When a cargo was due to land all concerned had a duty to perform. Farm labourers were marshalled in gangs and employed in collecting the smuggled goods from the beaches; farm wagons and carts, with teams of men and horses, were organised to collect the contraband, and farmers, millers, private people and even clerics prepared places in which to receive and hide the cargo; even the porch or belfry of the parish church was used as a store where goods awaited the arrival of other transport to carry them inland, Nobody saw anything wrong in these practices; the people involved were regarded as upright and respectable; the fact that they were engaged in the traffic was taken for granted. The only thing which was wrong was being caught and found out!

After a successful landing, when some of the farmer's horses had been borrowed during the night to pull the wagons or to act as pack horses for the transport of the cargo to its hiding place, there was generally a cask of spirits left somewhere for the Master or the Parson, and a few silks or ribbons for the lady: so sang Rudyard Kipling's *A Smuggler's Song*.

> If you wake at midnight and hear a horse's feet
> Don't go drawing back the blind, or looking down the
>   street.
> Them that asks no questions, isn't told a lie,
> Watch the wall, my darling, while the Gentlemen go by!
>
> Running round the woodlump if you chance to find
> Little barrels, roped and tarred, full of Brandy-wine
> Don't you shout to "Come and look", nor use them for
>   your play
> Put the brushwood back again, they'll be gone, next day.
>
> If you meet the Excise men, dressed in blue and red
> You be careful what you say; listen what is said;
> If they call you `pretty maid', and chuck you 'neath the
>   chin
> Don't you tell where no-one is; nor yet where no-one's
>   been.
>
> Five and twenty ponies trotting through the dark,
> Brandy for the Parson, 'Baccy for the Clerk,
> Laces for a lady, letters for a spy,
> Watch the wall, my darling, while the Gentlemen go by!

`Brandy for the Parson' was an actual and important part of these operations; many of the clerics had vested interests in what might be termed `un-holy Spirits'.

When Parson Ready was inducted to the Living at Warham he was told by his predecessor that he should get up early and open the front door of his Parsonage before daylight: if he found a keg of brandy outside it was a warning that he should not allow any-one, particularly strangers, to go into his barn for several days, as the smugglers had stored their goods inside. When, a few days later he should find a second keg, he would know that all the things had been removed. The Parson's barn was sacrosanct, and not likely to be raided.

There was no reason why `a present from a gentleman' should not be accepted. It was only a token of appreciation for some small, but valuable, act of co-operation, such as `forgetting' to lock the stable door at night. One Suffolk parson whose memory seemed to fail him in this way when a `run' was planned, was the Revd. Philip Meadows of Great Bealings. Small boat-loads of contraband could be rowed almost silently along Martlesham Creek, and the rowers would find the Parson's coach-house and stable unlocked. The waiting carriage was, of course, well-known in the district and those who saw it on the road would assume that the Vicar was engaged upon some nocturnal errand of mercy. When the bulky, but certainly not human, contents of the carriage had been safely deposited in their place of hiding the equipage would return to the Parsonage and the doors closed.

The Revd. James Woodforde, in his *Diary of a Country Parson*, a book giving a detailed account of the day-to-day life of a country cleric, has a number of illuminating references to the supply of smuggled spirits that came his way. Typical examples of the *Diary* entries are:

December 29, 1786. Had a Tub of Gin and another of Coniac brandy brought me this evening.

September 15. Had a Tub of Rum brought me this evening.

What is perhaps the most interesting entry is dated 17th May, 1780:

> I didn't go to bed till after 12 at night as I expected Richd. Andrews, the honest smuggler, with some Gin.

'The Honest Smuggler'! If ever there was a contradiction in terms it must be this. But then, such an appellation is but on a par with the sentiment expressed by Charles Lamb, when he wrote:

> I like a smuggler; he is the only honest thief. He robs nothing but the Revenue, an abstraction I never greatly care about.

Smugglers were clever, crafty and adapt at finding places in which to hide their contraband. While one cargo was being landed at Dunwich in 1790 a message which was always feared was brought to the leader of the gang - the Excise Men were on their way. An emergency plan, already conceived, was put into operation; a plan to lead the pack-horses through a lace-like pattern of by-ways and country lanes, some known only to local people, until they eventually arrived at the church at Westhall. There they found that the church roof was being re-thatched, and ladders were erected for work to proceed in the morning. This church had a double roof, and, relying upon the discretion of the thatchers, the smugglers laid their barrels in the valley of the roof, covered them with reeds, and left, knowing that they would be safe until their return.

A number of East Anglian churches were used for the temporary storage of smuggled goods. In a letter written by the poet Edward FitzGerald to Charles Keen, the writer refers to "... kegs of Hollands found under the altar cloth of Theberton Church"; while under the eaves of the chancel of the Church of Saint Edmund at Fritton can be seen a door through which the smugglers passed their goods to their hiding place in the roof. And not only in the roof. When repairs to the floor of St. Margaret's Church, Rishangles, were being carried out, a deep cavity was discovered which contained broken kegs and other evidence of goods being stored, which must have been with the knowledge of the Parson and/or the Clerk.

The runners also enlisted the help of innocents like Sally Bean, who lived in one of a pair of cottages which stood at the top of Shuck's Lane in Chelmondiston, from which position she could command an extensive view of the surrounding countryside. When she had grown old and was tinted brown of face from the smoke of a little short-stemmed clay pipe which she habitually smoked, she still received her keg of gin for keeping watch on the lanes for any sign of the Excise Officers. If she saw trouble coming she hobbled down the lane to the foreshore to raise the alarm. On one occasion it is said Sally saw the Servants of the Law approaching, just as she had received her keg. The Officers, who had had her constantly under suspicion, searched her cottage but "... there she squatted on her keg, with her skirts drawn down over it, an' they never did find it."

The foregoing may be construed as a record of what might be describe as domestic or small-time smuggling; the real events were different. Carried out by organised gangs, the prizes were larger and consequently the risks were greater, so that violence and bloodshed often occurred. Margaret Catchpole's story involved killings and murder, and many were the reports of similar happenings. The local newspapers, including the *Ipswich Journal*, and the *Gentleman's Magazine*, were full of accounts of skirmishes and even pitched battles between the smugglers and the Dragoons, as the former attempted to unload their illegal freight.

The beach at Sizewell is today completely over-shadowed by the Nuclear Power Station, but not so much altered that it is impossible to imagine what it looked like in the olden days. Behind the pebbly beach lies the wide, flat area of coarse grass, with series of hummocks and undulations, still largely undisturbed. quiet and peaceful. It is not difficult to envisage pack-horses standing in the background, silent waiting in the hours of darkness, with wagons drawn up on the well-worn stony track, ready to be loaded and to rumble away.

That is the peaceful scene at Sizewell; the other is different.

This is the arena where many a desperate encounter took place between the Officers of the Crown and the contraband runners.

The beach at Sizewell was used by others than the local men; the 'Hadleigh Gang' left its beach stained with blood on more than one occasion. To realise the ferocity of their encounters with the Excise Men, consider the report of one incident in 1775. The smugglers did not always have matters their own way. On 23rd February of that year a party of Dragoons captured six wagons leaving Sizewell beach and found them to contain barrels of Spirits, and on 2nd March the soldiers had an even greater success and seized forty horses and fifteen carts loaded with spirituous liquors, tea and draperies. These successes on the part of the Authorities were not without their price being paid. Violence erupted and tragedy followed with the deaths of a number of men on both sides.

The 'Hadleigh Gang' was one of the largest and most ruthless of the gangs of smugglers on the East Coast. They appear to have been principally employed with the illegal importing of tea and dry goods, although there is no doubt that, at times, they carried spirits and tobacco as well. It is known that in 1745 they made at least four landings at Sizewell, one involving the use of eighty horses. Such an operation would involve a great deal of detailed planning, but their organisation was superb, as it had to be, to operate from a beach at Sizewell when their base was thirty-five miles away inland. How long it took to convey their contraband by pack-horse and waggon from the sea to Hadleigh is a matter for conjecture; they must have had various hideaways and resting places along the route.

Some of the tea reaching Hadleigh was stored in a cottage at Semer, a nearby village, and the discovery of this hoard by the Dragoons ended in a pitched battle in which one soldier was killed and men on both sides were injured.

As the result of a number of similar incidents involving loss of life, the Commissioners of Customs, in July, 1732, drew the attention of the Treasury to the "... extent of Smuggling in

Suffolk" and petitioned for an increase in the number of soldiers stationed along the coast "... to assist the Customs Officers in overcoming the trade." A somewhat delayed result of this request materialised thirty-two years later: in 1764 parties of Dragoons were stationed at Stowmarket, Woodbridge, Saxmundham and Walton "... in order to check the proceedings of the Smugglers".

At the close of the Napoleonic Wars the effectiveness of the Revenue Service was greatly increased. A 'Coastal Blockade' was established in 1816, whereby troops from ships patrolling at sea were set ashore at sunset to patrol the beaches during the night, returning aboard at dawn. The system, however, was not entirely satisfactory and was abolished in 1831. Having been established by the Customs Department in 1822, the Coast Guard Service was intensified, and eventually handed over to the Admiralty in 1856.

DISCOVERY BY THE DEBEN

One of the greatest archæological digs in the annals of British history, with no parallel in any other part of the country, took place in the centre of 'Catchpole Country'.

On a plateau which rises steeply from the river flats on the bank of the River Deben there lie a group of ancient burial mounds which have been excavated and produced some historic treasures. A series of modern organised excavations began in 1938 and proved that the mounds had been plundered before, and many of their contents had been removed. The next year, work began in earnest to discover what the mounds still contained, and yielded exciting and unexpected results. The excavating party found a magnificent Ship Burial, containing articles of remarkable wealth and historic interest, causing them to conclude that this was the burial place of Rædwald, King of East Anglia, who died in the year 624.

The group of mounds was first recorded in 1601 by the cartographer, John Norden, while producing a survey of the district. They were noted again in 1629 on a survey of the Sutton parish; and on a larger survey covering the whole of Suffolk they appeared again in 1783. They were first described as `tumuli' in 1836, and an Ordnance Survey of 1889 describes a `Cemetery' with ten mounds on the site.

The first recorded dig in the `cemetery' was in 1860, a somewhat `light-hearted' adventure by a group of ratings from a Naval survey craft which was moored in the Deben. They discovered "... two bushels of nails" which were eventually given to a local blacksmith. In 1938 Mrs Edith Pretty, who owned the estate upon which the site was situated approached Basil Brown, a local archæologist, with the suggestion that he should lead a team to properly excavate the mounds. This was arranged, and Brown and his assistants began by opening one of the smaller mounds, where he found cremated bones of a man and a horse, together with a bronze lid, a chain and an axe. The excavation of a second mound yielded various personal items including the point of a sword, a silver buckle, a bronze ring and the blades of a knife. Although robbed previously it was still possible to identify this as the place of burial of a young man; some of whose bones were there with those of his horse.

In 1939 work commenced on opening the largest of the group of mounds. Brown's first find was an iron rivet which had obviously been used in the construction of a ship. Eventually, after very careful digging, the ship emerged. Naturally, the wood originally used in its construction had not survived; all that was left, after the infilling sand had been painstakingly removed, was an extremely fragile impression formed from a thin crust of sand, hardened by being compressed by the wood which had given it shape. The rivets remained in the sand exactly in their original positions, and outline depressions showing the plank runs could easily be seen.

When finally uncovered the ship measured approximately ninety feet in length with a maximum beam of fourteen feet. She was a huge open boat, propelled by forty oarsmen and guided by a steering paddle. There was no evidence to suggest that a mast had been fitted or a sail used.

The centre of the ship was occupied by a large Burial Chamber within which a resplendent pagan burial had been arranged; providing the deceased with all the resources he might require for every aspect of life in the After-world. Personal Possessions were comprehensively provided and laid out; domestic requirements were not forgotten. There was an iron-bound tub of yew-tree wood standing beside a smaller bucket, a large Anastasius dish lay near a silver bowl containing cups spear heads and knives with bone handles. The remains of a mass of textiles and various accoutrements were piled on the floor.

There was a lamp, bottles, spears and a variety of other weapons, together with a whetstone and a sword with jewelled pommel and golden hilt. Perhaps the most spectacular find of all was a shield and a helmet. The shield was made of limewood and covered with hide. A bronze strip, clipped to the rim enclosed delicate decorations in gilt-bronze, representing animals, while the centre was occupied by a skilfully decorated iron and bronze knob. By delicate restoration work the helmet, which had been crushed by falling timbers, has now been restored to its original shape, revealing that it is indeed a thing of beauty, a remarkable example of the expertise of a metalsmith. Forged from a single piece of iron, it has iron ear-flaps and a bronze neck-guard. It has an oval iron face-mask, with a realistic nose and mouth made of gilded bronze. Cast bronze eyebrows are inlaid with silver, their terminals representing a boar's head.

The helmet has similarities with those buried in the graves of Chieftains in Sweden. There, in the 6th and 7th centuries, the Chiefs of Regions were buried in ships, accompanied by the wealth which was theirs during their lifetime. Their helmets were remarkably similar to the Sutton Hoo helmet, but, while the Swedish warriors' headgear was made from sections of iron strips, the British helmet was forged from a single sheet of iron.

But the ship buried and unearthed at Sutton Hoo held no body, nor had it done so: the excavators were convinced that while such personal items as shoes, buckles and folded clothing abounded, they had never clothed a person and moreover, there was no trace of bones or teeth or any sign that a body had ever been there.

So, was this the grave of Rædwald; or was it a 7th century cenotaph?

One explanation may be found in the known behaviour of Rædwald himself. During a visit he paid to Kent he professed to have embraced the Christian Faith and adopted the Christian practices in religious observance, but on returning home to East Anglia, probably to Rendlesham, he reverted to the worship of the pagan gods. If this Ship Burial was prepared as his pagan tomb, it is possible that, secretly, soon after his death, his body was given a Christian burial. The ship would then be buried as his memorial, and as those who did so believed, be ready for his use in another world. The truth of the matter will never be known.

A Coroner's Treasure Trove inquest upon the contents of the grave was held in 1939 and they were awarded to Mrs. Pretty, who, with great generosity, presented them to the British Museum.

The discovery of the Sutton Hoo Burial Ship has been linked with the great Anglo-Saxon poem, *Beowulf*, recognised as "... the greatest poem to come from the first thousand years of our literary history". It has been described as "... a national monument as well as a poem". Two passages from *Beowulf* were read in the Coroner's Court when the ownership of the Sutton Hoo treasure was being decided; One described a ship burial - that of Scyld Scefing, a hero of the Scyldings, or Danes, who arrived mysteriously in a boat as a boy, and was appropriately buried in a boat when he died. The poem says that he was buried "... deep within the ring-prowed boat" and that "... many treasures and adornments were gathered there".

The other extract from the poem which was read at the Inquest was part of the description of the burial of Beowulf:

They buried rings and brooches -

All those adornments that brave men had;

71

They bequeathed the gleaming gold
Treasure of men
To the earth.

The Sutton Hoo burial could be described in the same terms.

This does two things: it shows that the Court of an East Anglian King was uniquely sophisticated. Such priceless treasures as an enormous gold buckle, the lid of a purse jewelled with garnets, gold shoulder-clasps also inlaid with garnets, and many other treasures, all point to wealth and sophistication; while, what is a remarkable fact which demands consideration, every artifact had its counterpart in *Beowulf*.

The second thing which emerges is the establishment of definite links between the Wuffing dynasty and the Royal House of Sweden.

Two characters in *Beowulf* are of special interest. One is Offa of Angeln, the 4th century King of the Angles, whose descendent and namesake, Offa, reigned in Mercia from 757 to 796; the other Hengest, who succeeded Hnaef as a leader among the Danes, and who traditionally came to Britain with another leader, Horsa, in 449 at the invitation of King Vortigern to fight against the Picts.

This is the Hengest who, according to the *Anglo Saxon Chronicle*, then turned his sword against Vortigern and the Britons, and established his own Kingdom in Kent, thus becoming the first Anglo-Saxon settler in England.

The geographical background of *Beowulf* lies in Sweden and Denmark, particularly the former, but connections with Britain cannot be ruled out. References to battles and the intermingling of characters known to both countries makes it possible that there may well have been a common ancestry between the two dynasties. If this is so, the unknown author of *Beowulf* could have been retailing some of the legendary history of the peoples of the Northern Hemisphere. It looks as though the writer of the poem was well acquainted with the Burial at Sutton Hoo, and it brings to one's notice once again the similarity of the names `Ulfketel' and `Wolfkettle' as quoted by Cobbold, with `Wuffing' 'Beowulf' and 'Offa'.

How significant is the pointer to a Swedish - British connection ?

THE MYSTERY OF SHINGLE STREET

And by the tide alone the water swayed,
Stealthy withdrawings, interminglings mild
Of light and shade in beauty reconciled,
Such is the prospect, far as eye can see. (Wordsworth)

When, in the 5th century, the Romans withdrew their garrisons from along the Saxon Shore, the Suffolk coast lay open to the invasions by the Angles and Saxons, against whom it had previously been guarded. By the year 500 these tribes were firmly established, having cleared the forests and made homes in the clearings. The many names ending with `ley' indicate where these settlements were made, such as at Hollesley and Trimley.

Many of these places did not develop into towns, Hollesley in particular remaining a small quiet place, surrounded by heather-covered heath-land, and looking towards the sea-fringed marshes.

On a shelving beach, washed regularly by the tide, stands a Martello Tower, a lonely sentinel, symbol of "... wars and rumours of wars" of days gone by. This long, wide pebble beach, while undoubtedly the scene of what Wordsworth termed "...battles long ago", especially between the smugglers and the Excise Men, is believed by many to have been the scene of more awful encounters in modern times. As already noted, it was expected that Napoleon would attempt an invasion at this part of the Suffolk coast; now history becomes contemporary by repeating itself in the 20th century.

The summer of 1940 was filled with rumours: word was passed from person to person that a Nazi invasion of England was imminent, and fear and foreboding filled the hearts of the population, in particular those living on the East Coast. The place where this landing of German troops was to take place was pin-pointed as Shingle Street on Hollesley Bay, where the terrain was eminently suitable for such action.

Then came stories that such an invasion had been attempted, and accounts of terrible happenings were in circulation. Although the incidental elaborations of the `information' varied, the central `facts' of the stories told and re-told were generally the same; that a force of German Commando Troops, dressed as British soldiers, had landed at Shingle Street one night in the summer of 1940, but were repulsed by British forces. It was further asserted that the raid was aimed at an attack on the top-secret radar research station at Bawdsey Manor nearby. To make the `evidence' realistic it was further stated that such was the slaughter of the invading forces that Winston Churchill ordered that the dead should be buried in a communal grave-pit in nearby Rendlesham Forest.

The whole of East Anglia, and, indeed, much of the country, was alive with rumours. In spite of the fact that all the people living near Shingle Street had been evacuated, there circulated what claimed to be `eye witness' accounts of what took place. One Coastguard claimed that he had been ordered to "... look out for charred bodies in the sea"; another spoke of "... terrible things that had been hushed up; yet another, an intelligence officer, said that he arrived on the shore to find "... the shingle covered with bodies charred beyond recognition but wearing British uniforms". The same man claimed that he found on the shingle a burned-out dinghy bearing German markings, and that he was told by a senior officer that he had never seen it, that it was to be removed immediately, and that the whole incident had never happened. To give the rumours some sort of credence, a Royal Marine sergeant was reported to have said that "... the beach was covered with bodies, and the whole sea was ablaze."

To explain the gruesome stories of `charred bodies' and the `sea on fire', it was said that the British Ministry of Defence, in an attempt to find a reliable anti-invasion weapon, had developed a system of under-water pipes which spread kerosene - petrol and heavy oil - on the water, and ignited them with calcium phosphorus; thus causing what was described as a `flame barrier'. The invading force, bombed from the air, were caught in this holocaust, with the result described.

That something did happen at Shingle Street is beyond doubt; and it is equally certain that the matter was hushed up. But why? Secrets can be kept for a very long time, but after fifty years it is a mystery why certain Government Departments rule that their files on this matter are still secret.

In 1992 a writer in the *East Anglian Daily Times* asked why this secrecy persisted and aroused a considerable correspondence in both the local and the national press, including some revealing statements from elderly people who claimed to have been involved in the happenings. The new public pressure to be told the truth thus engendered resulted in the Home Secretary and the local Member of Parliament being empowered to make public some of the relevant files, but not all of them; the others, it was determined, were to remain secret.

The production of such files as were made public gave the information that the evacuation of Shingle Street was necessary for mines to be laid on the Strand, and that nothing much else happened. But, if that is all that took place, why has it been necessary to decide that this cannot be public knowledge for seventy-five years? Reading between what `lines' there are available, it would appear that there is much more to be revealed, and that there is at least an element of truth in many of the stories which have circulated.

The riddle of Shingle Street remains unsolved, and the persistent desire for its solution refuses to be silenced. Was there an attempted invasion? Some say `yes', others deny it.

There is one question which needs to be answered, because to do so may very well give the answer to the whole. For what purpose were those train-loads of `quick-lime' sent hurtling through the night toward the Suffolk coast?

They were not phantom trains!

THE FIVE TOWNS OF SOLE BAY

ALDEBURGH

There is no sea like the Aldeburgh sea;

"It speaks to me", wrote Edward FitzGerald. It has `spoken' to many people in many voices, often with the voice of aggression! The ancient 16th century Moot Hall standing on the edge of the waves is proof of what George Crabbe had in mind when he wrote

"... the ocean roar
 Whose greedy waves devour the lessening shore."

The original town, of which the Moot Hall was the centre, is no more; the sea, from whom the town's inhabitants wrested their wealth has reclaimed all they had taken from it.

The beach is littered with boats of all kinds, many belonging to the local fishermen who sell their catches direct from their boats after landing, or from partly tumble-down little wooden shacks on the pebbles: they find ready customers, for Aldeburgh is famous for `long-shore' herring and sprats in season. The Lifeboat stands poised, ready to swoop down the slips into the breakers when there is a need. To the south of the promenade the River Alde; which further south becomes the Ore runs parallel to the tide line; in this quiet river are the moorings of the popular Yacht Club, and between the river and the sea the guarding omnipotence of the most northerly Martello Tower in East Anglia.

At the end of the 19th century the popularity of Aldeburgh as a watering place slumped, and the town experienced a very quiet period; but in 1948 a dramatic change took place when Benjamin Britten founded the Aldeburgh Festival of Music and the Arts and built a new concert hall at Snape Maltings. Today crowds of music-lovers have restored prosperity to the town and district: in the `season' accommodation is impossible to obtain unless booked at least a year in advance and the popularity of Aldeburgh as a holiday resort has increased considerably. One cannot help but think again of Crabbe who described the holiday-makers thus:

The Moot Hall, Aldeburgh

Snape Maltings

"Soon as the season comes, the crowds arrive To their superior rooms the wealthy arrive; Others look round for lodgings snug and small. The brick-floored parlour which the butcher lets". It has not been verified whether modern `butchers' have a "...brick-floored parlour", but the crowds certainly pour in.

DUNWICH

These days there is not much to see at Dunwich, but there is much to ponder; for once again, as at Aldeburgh, the visitor is in the presence of the encroaching sea. It is an `Old, old story', for even the writers of Domesday had to report that the sea had eaten away (*mare abstulit*) one third of the Carucates. "As much land as a team can plough in a year" (Nuttall) of cultivated land accredited to the town. So it has gone on: villages and hamlets have, like the town of Dunwich, disappeared beneath the conquering waves.

But the history of Dunwich is worth remembering. After the occupying Roman Legions passed, their Station became a centre for Saxon influence. In the 6th century Christianity became established in East Anglia when Saint Felix was created the first Bishop of Dunwich, establishing a See, and crowning Sigebert as King of the Eastern Angles. Sigebert built a palace at Dunwich in 630, which was at some time occupied by Rædwald who, in his other palace at Rendlesham, erected two altars, one to his pagan gods and one to the God of the Christians. This is the Rædwald believed to be commemorated in the Ship Burial at Sutton Hoo.

Dunwich became powerful and prosperous and a Dominican Monastery arose, and another of Friars Minor. There was a Norman Lazer Hospital, a Church of the Knights Templar, nine churches and three lesser chapels. Beside ecclesiastical prosperity the town advanced in wealth also, becoming larger in extent and greater in the number of inhabitants that Ipswich. Its maritime trade prospered through the importance of its position as a port.

All this is now buried beneath the waves: it is an area of

legend and superstition, folk-lore and tales of supernatural ghosts and apparitions. Fishermen sailing home on the evening tide say that sometimes they hear the bells of lost churches, the lowing of drowned cattle, and all the sounds of the countryside coming from under the waves. There is little of Dunwich left: what there is lives in fear of a fate which may overtake it when the north-easter blows up a gale once more.

The mystery and tragedy of Dunwich has always activated people's imagination. Authors have involved its history in the basis of their stories; historians have delved deep into the past to comment on the horror of the facts as they saw them; and poets have been both sentimental and stirring in their rhymes. Algernon Charles Swinburne's lines describing the ruins of the Church of All Saints sum it up:

"... one hollow tower and hoary,
Naked in the sea-wind, stands and moans,
Filled and thrilled with its perpetual story,
Where earth is dense with dead men's bones".

WALBERSWICK

Walberswick occupies an attractive position at the mouth of the tidal River Blyth. The original quays at the estuary, once the scenes of great activity, are now empty and derelict, but the river is full of moored fishing and sailing boats; while the great 15th century church, now but a ruin of its former self, overlooks the marshland and extensive heathland, delightful in all seasons.

The Church has a famous tower, built in 1426 by two men who, after finding all the materials necessary for building the whole church were paid forty shillings and a cade (cask) of five-hundred herrings per annum.

Walberswick parish church was a noble building, but, like so many others erected in East Anglia, was far too large for local requirements, and in 1695 permission was granted to demolish all excepting the tower, the porch and the south aisle, and sell the materials against the cost of refurbishing those parts of the original building which remained. These remnants of former glory are what remain today.

BLYTHBURGH

Visitors who wish to proceed further along the shore of Sole Bay may be able to persuade a Walberswick fisherman to row them across the River Blyth; if not, they must walk a mile up-stream to a footbridge which was once a bridge on the defunct Southwold to Halesworth Railway. The first bridge for vehicles which crosses the river is at Blythburgh itself.

Tidal waters come right up to Blythburgh, where there are the scant remains of a town once much larger and of far greater importance. There were busy wharves where ships docked for an important fish trade and for the export of woollen cloth in connection with the flourishing weaving industry. But now no more. As ships were built of deeper draught they became too big to reach the river dockside, and trade fell away. What had been a bustling port became the village of today; although, with its old houses and its renowned White Hart Inn there is still much to attract visitors in large numbers.

The White Hart Inn, which in its history has played many parts in the life of the community, including that of being a Court House, bears witness to the influence of men from the Netherlands, because of its Dutch gables, as in other local buildings. These men may have been Flemish weavers who came to teach the Englishmen in the art of manufacturing 'Bays and Sayes'; or they could have been engaged in draining the marshes, as at Earith and Denver; or, again, they could have been Huguenot refugees who had fled to England for the sake of religious liberty. Why they were here is of no great importance: suffice it to say that once here, they stayed, and left their mark in East Anglia, not least in the beauty of the buildings they erected.

The great attraction to Blythburgh is its church. Viewed from a distance across the marshes, it is one of the grandest sights in the district. While it is about one hundred and thirty feet long, it has about it a gracefulness which proclaims the skill and devotion of its 15th century builders. It is also a witness to the great wealth enjoyed by the people of the district five centuries ago.

SOUTHWOLD

Upon a low cliff, overlooking the sea and the Blyth Estuary, stands Southwold, a town which is attractive in every way, its lay-out may well have been an early attempt at town planning, as it evolved after a disastrous fire in 1659 which destroyed practically the whole of the town which stood there before. There are open 'Greens' surrounded by many good Georgian houses and an interesting High Street which leads into a Market Place where Morris Dancers sometimes perform for the entertainment of summer visitors. The fine Swan Hotel cannot go un-noticed. Adjacent to the Town Hall, and diagonally across from the Old Gaol, the Swan looks backwards over its shoulder at the towers of the Church and the Lighthouse. From almost every window there is a fascinating panorama down the narrow streets or out to sea.

For centuries this hotel has held an important place in the life of Southwold. Destroyed in the great fire of 1659, and re-built, it was remodelled in 1820, with further suitable alterations and additions in more recent years. Today it is a classic seaside hotel in one of the most delightful towns in England.

On Gun Cliff, the sea-ward limit of one of Southwold's beautiful Greens, stand six eighteen-pounder guns, carrying the emblem of the Tudor Rose and the Crown. They are said to have been captured by Bonnie Prince Charlie during the rising of '45 and used by his army at the disastrous Battle of Culloden when he was finally defeated. The guns were re-captured by the Duke of Cumberland's army, and later presented by the Duke to Southwold on the suggestion of the King because the town had petitioned him for defences, as they were in fear of invasion by the Dutch.

In the early days Southwold was renowned for its fishery and its fleet of fishing boats, square-rigged herring smacks. Defoe records that in his day the only industry in Southwold, or 'Swole', as local pronunciation rendered it, was "... the curing of sprats", an occupation which was eventually transferred to Yarmouth along with the curing of herrings.

Domesday shows that Southwold was obliged to honour an annual rental payment of twenty-five thousand herring to the Lord of the Manor. The survey also reveals that the town had a 'sea-weir', a wicker-work fence built under the water to entrap the fish when it was too rough to go out in boats; as the lines of an old song seem to indicate:

"Weir fish for Wednesday; swell the net full"; another song supports the story that, in those sailing days, whether they launched their boats or not depended upon the state of the wind. It is said that when a fisherman awoke in the morning he would open his window and hold a lighted candle outside. If there was enough wind to extinguish the flame, it was too rough to sail: if there was not enough to do so, there was not enough by which to sail, so he went back to bed.

"So I open the pane, and pop out the flame, To see how the wind do blow" (believe that if you like!).

In the 16th century it was hoped that Southwold would rise in importance when attempts were made to build a harbour and create a port which was designed to out-rival Harwich; steal the Continental traffic; and, at the same time, bring back to the town the herring industry which had been appropriated by the Dutch. In association with these plans the Free British Fishery Company was created in 1750, but it ceased trading fifty years later, and the whole idea of expansion was eventually abandoned.

On this part of the East Coast a wind blowing from the north-east will cause the rush of sea-water to carry a carpet of fine sand from the Yarmouth Banks, and pile it up off Southwold. When the wind shifts, the sand is dragged away again, leaving a ridge of pebbles (to local people the tide is either 'making' or 'scouring'). This tidal action was the main reason for attempts to build a harbour at Southwold being abandoned: and, although from time to time there have been subsequent revivals of the idea, none of them has come to fruition.

In the year 1880 the Little Railway, operated by a private company, reached Southwold. This narrow-gauge line carried passengers, commercial traffic and coal from Halesworth to Southwold, and holiday passengers, their luggage, fish and milk churns on the return journey. The line was, however, expensive to operate and, because of its narrow gauge, the rolling stock could go no further than Halesworth, therefore everything it carried destined for a further destination had to be man-handled on to the trains of the Great Eastern Railway. The life-time of the Halesworth - Southwold Railway was only half a century.

There is now no harbour, the sea being master of the situation; and no railway. Small fishing boats ply their trade from Buss Creek, where there flourishes an active Yacht Club.

The Sole Bay Lighthouse was built in 1899. Those responsible for the erection of this gleaming white tower were taking no chances! With so much of the original town under the sea, and knowing that coastal erosion was still a hazard, they positioned their building away from the cliffs, on a site in the town centre.

The finest mediæval possession of Southwold is its parish church of cathedral-like proportions and majestic beauty. In a county famous for the number and excellence of its churches, the Church of Saint Edmund at Southwold is outstanding. The magnificent windows, mediæval tower and splendid porch magnify the wonders of a building one hundred and forty four feet long; where the roof of the nave is a masterpiece of the wood-carver's art, with angels adorning the hammer-beams. The stalls of the chancel are richly carved angels and trumpeters adorn the organ, and the mediæval pulpit draws the attention of all eyes. Added to this, none can miss 'Jack-o'-the-Clock', a four foot high figure dressed in the armour of the Wars of the Roses, who strikes the hour-bell with his weapons. The first religious building to be

83

The lighthouse and green, Southwold

erected on the site of Saint Edmund's Church was a chapel, built in 1202, when Jocelin Brakelond was Lord of the Manor. The present building was erected 1430-60; additions completed twenty years later.

THE SOLE BAY LAZER HOUSE

That there should be a Lazer House at Dunwich is a matter of great interest. Lazer Houses were named after Lazarus, the beggar who was laid at the gate of a certain rich man in the hope that of his riches the owner would have compassion on the one who was dying of leprosy (*St. Luke*).

Leprosy has been a dreaded disease from as far back as records can be traced. As long ago as the giving of the Jewish Law in the Pentateuch leprosy was recognised as a disease to be feared. The Book *Leviticus* alone has several chapters which deal with the ways in which to distinguish it and how to deal with it and to treat those who suffer from it. Segregation, it was considered, was the answer; a course of action adopted, not with the hope of curing the patient, but of stopping the spread of a parasitic plague.

The Jewish leper was instructed to "... rend his garments" and to proceed along his way with a mournful cry of "Unclean; unclean!" (*Leviticus* XIII); and centuries later, in the mediæval days of Merrie England, the same penalty was placed upon sufferers, who had to dress in a grey gown and loudly announce their coming by either ringing a bell or with clappers.

In the Middle Ages there were more than ninety Leper Hospices in England; one well known in East Anglia the Lazer House of Saint Mary Magdalen at Stourbridge, Cambridge, where the Chapel of the Hospital still stands. There is no record of the date of the foundation of Dunwich's Lazer House; or anything to say by whom it was established. The first evidence of its existence comes in some sort of litigation whereby the Hospital Authorities fought for and gained ownership of "... A tenement in Comberton", with which they had been endowed, but of which they had been somehow deprived by one, Alan de Berton. This legal action took place in the King's Court in 1193. Twenty-one years later King John granted the Hospice `A Feir... to be held in the close of the Hospital on the vigil and feast of the Holy Cross yearly'. It may well be that this was the origin of what became the famous Stourbridge Fair.

Records concerning the work of the Cambridge Hospital for Lepers do not exist, apart from some remarks concerning its appreciation; but it is known that in 1272 the Burgesses complained that the Warden was not caring for as many lepers as he should do. At that time the then Bishop of Ely sought and gained control of the institution; this was so held in Bishopric hands until the Hospital was abolished by Henry VIII. When that happened the Chapel was presented to Cambridge University, and was renovated in 1867 under the direction of Sir Gilbert Scott.

Generally the inmates of leper hospitals were tended by Anglican monks and friars of the Dominican and Franciscan Orders, devoted men who gave themselves completely to providing as much comfort as possible to the afflicted. The protection and care thus given by the Church ranks among the most Divine-like of its actions. Even so, in the public mind, anyone pronounced a leper in England had already died; for those who were not cared for in Lazer Houses were cast out from society in accordance, it was said, with the implicit instructions to do so contained in the Old Testament. The passage of Scripture which was quoted as authority reads:

> And the Lord spake unto Moses, saying; Command the Children of Israel that they put out of the camp every leper, both male and female shall ye put out, without the camp shall ye put them. (*Numbers*)

It comes as a shock in this century to realise that this practice persisted into the `enlightened' years of the Christian Dispensation: but the Ritual for the Sequestration of a Leper, which had great similarity to the Service for the Burial of the Dead, still remains and speaks for itself! This is part of it. Met at the door of the Church by the Priest, the leper was sprinkled with Holy Water, then conducted into the building to hear Mass. At the conclusion of that Office the Priest conducted his Charge to a wooden hut which had been erected in an extremely isolated position, where the leper was to spend the remainder of his days. At the door of the hut the Priest pronounced:

"I forbid you entering the Church or entering the company of others. I forbid you quitting your home without your leper's dress. You are not to be indignant at being thus separated from others, as to your little wants, good people will provide for you, and God will not desert you. When it shall come to pass that the leper shall pass out of this world, he shall be buried in his hut and not in the Churchyard." Fancy a man, critically ill, standing and hearing that! At one time there was concern expressed about the consequent separation of husbands and wives; it was asked, should the man with leprosy be isolated alone? The Church ruled that marriage is indissoluble, and wives were then allowed, if they wished, to enter into banishment with their husbands. One of the greatest tragic poems of all time is Tennyson's 'The Leper's Bride'; it stirs the emotions and gives a vivid portrayal of things as they were. Its twenty-seven verses begin :

> Why wail you, pretty plover? and what is it that you fear?
> Is he sick your mate like mine? have you lost him, is he
> fled?
> And there - the heron rises from his watch beside the
> mere,
> And flies above the leper's hut, where lives the living-dead.

In England the disease is eradicated; and in those countries where it still ravages the population, great efforts are made to see that the sufferers are being cared for.

THE KNIGHTS TEMPLAR

John Day, the historian printer of Dunwich, the first English printer to use Saxon type, in his *History* of that town, described the local Knight's Church as:

"... an aunchent and verie old church called the Temple: the which church by report was in the Jews' time."

This was one of the remarkable round churches built by the Templars; others being St Sepulchre's at Northampton (1100); Little Maplestead (c.1300); the Temple Church, London (1185); the Chapel at Ludlow Castle (c.1120); and the Church of the Holy Sepulchre and Saint Andrew in Cambridge (1120).

Day's reference to "... the Jews" seems to refer to those of that race who aided and established the commercial and financial prosperity of Norwich.

The origin of Norwich is obscure: `Wic' means `a settlement', so probably a village which had sprung on the North bank of the River Wensum, where the Roman road from Caister crossed the water, was given that name by joining `North' and `Wic' together.

By 925 the town was sufficiently important to mint its own coins which it did until 1250. In 1065 there was a population of "... 5,000 souls", among whom were a strong colony of Jews from Normandy. They occupied an area around White Lion Street, becoming both populous and prosperous. The Knights Templar were closely associated with them, particularly in their prosperity.

It is significant that the Templar's Church in Cambridge was erected in `... the Jewry'. That part of the University Town so described lay between the old church of All Saints and the Knight's Church; an area that Thomas Atkins described in his monumental volume *Cambridge described and illustrated* (1892) in these terms:

All to the East of Conduit Street, the present Sidney Street, was occupied by the Benedictine Nuns and the Franciscan Friars. To the west of Trinity Street lay some waste ground. The bulk of the inhabitants lived in the area between these two thoroughfares... this area formed the Jewry...

There seems little doubt but that at the time of the settlement of the Jews, both in Norwich and Cambridge, the Knights were associated with, if not instrumental in what happened there.

Their's was an aristocratic Lay Order, which accrued such riches and strength that it became feared by clergy and laity alike, because it was believed that the members profited from their involvement in the practice of witchcraft.

The Knights observed absolute secrecy concerning their affairs, equalled only by the Masonic crafts of today, although their philosophy was based upon the Rules compiled by Saint Bernard of Clairvaux for the monks of the Cistercian Order. Without doubt it was this secrecy which caused the inquisitive non-members of the Order to speculate and circulate weird tales and superstitions about them.

So great did the power exercised by the Templar Knights over the community become that a Papal Bull concerning their activities was issued by Pope Innocent II in 1139. By this they were given permission to build their own places of prayer, which permission eventuated in the erection of the round Templar Churches. By the same Bull they were allowed to claim exemption from tithes and to appoint their own Priests. They were also granted permission to have and administer their own burial places and ordinances.

It was these burial rites which caused ordinary members of the population to turn against the Knights. They were accused of dabbling in the occult, and of heresy. The particular heretical behaviour which disturbed, indeed frightened, the ordinary citizens was the practice of exhuming their dead after they had been buried for three years and dividing their bones into several parts, then re-interring each part in a separate place.

So great did the public opposition to the Knights become that the Order was suppressed by Pope Clement in 1312. The final accusation levelled against them, which caused their suppression, was that they renounced Christ, and spat upon the Holy Cross.

The angel roof at Blythburgh

ANNA, ETHELREDA and WITHBURGA

Historians pay special attention to the Church at Blythburgh because a King was buried in a former building on that consecrated site.

According to the *Liber Eliensis* (*Ely Chronicle*) in 654 a great battle was fought where Blythburgh stands, between King Anna and Penda, King of Mercia, and Anna was slain. The Venerable Bede tells in his *Ecclesiastica Brittanica* that "Anna was a good man" who had "... good and pious offspring". He founded a monastery at Blythburgh and embellished that founded by the Irish monk Fursa at Burgh Castle.

Anna's palace was one of those of the Wuffinga dynasty, situated at Exning, from where he conducted his defensive campaigns against the marauding armies of Penda, the last of which led to the Battle of Bulcamp Hill when Anna was slain. He was buried at Blythburgh, but later his body was removed to Ely where his daughter, Ethelreda, had founded a convent.

Ethelreda was born at Exning and baptized by Felix, Bishop of Dunwich, in a natural spring known as Saint Mindred's Well. This spring, once a centre for pilgrimage, still runs in land which is part of Newmarket's racing world.

In her youth Ethelreda made a vow of perpetual virginity. Her first husband, Tonbert, accepted and honoured her wishes; but while her second husband, Egfrid, whom she married five years after Tonbert's death, agreed to do so when their marriage was new, he changed his mind after inheriting his father's throne in Northumbria in 670. Desiring an heir, he tried to make his wife break her vow: she refused and stormy disputes ended in divorce.

Seeking the safety of cloistered walls did not save Ethelreda from her husband's wrath; he pursued her, but she fled south to an island in the Fens, now called Ely, where she built a retreat for any like her who were being persecuted. After establishing a convent, and living as Abbess for six years, she fell victim of the plague, and died.

Ethelreda was succeeded as Abbess by her sister Sexburgh; while two more of Anna's 'pious offspring' pursued the same holy path; Athelburg becoming Abbess of Bric, in France, and Withburga founding a Convent at East Dereham in Norfolk. It is with East Dereham that Withburga will for ever be associated; she not only founded her Religious Order, she also built a Church. The Abbey and the Church were subsequently destroyed by invading Danes, but the attention which these foundations had gathered was no doubt instrumental in forming the beginnings of the town which eventually developed around them.

After her death in 654 Withburga was buried in the church-yard, but later re-interred within the church. So great was her renown that pilgrims in increasing numbers visited her tomb where miracles of healing were reported to take place. Consequently buildings sprung up for the accommodation of these pilgrims, and in the supply of their necessities and the organisation of their hospitality lay the commercial foundation of the community.

The elaborate town sign which now spans the main street acknowledges the influence of Withburga's Abbey in the foundation of Dereham. The town's name is derived from two does which, legend asserts, came to the convent regularly to be milked at a time when the Institution was in dire financial difficulties, having no money and no food. These deer are depicted on the Sign, as is also the huntsman who endeavoured to kill them. Between the man and the deer stands an angel, blocking the man's path so securing the survival of the Religious House.

The continued presence of Withburga's remains as a point of pilgrimage would, doubtless, have added greatly to the prosperity of the town; but this was not to be. In the year 974 the Abbot of Ely, jealous of the prosperity that the pilgrimages to Dereham was bringing to the town, came with a company of Monks and, while the Abbot was entertaining the Burgers, to a feast, the monks stole the body of Withburga and took it away. They were pursued by the men of Dereham who were unable to catch them because the wily monks, having reached the sanctuary of the Fen waters took boat and escaped across the flood.

Withburga's remains were buried at Ely beside those of her sainted sisters, Ethelreda, Sexburga and Werburga.

At East Dereham a vaulted chamber in the Churchyard bears the inscription:

'The ruins of a tomb which contained the Remains of Withburga - youngest daughter of Annas, King of the Eastern Angles, - who died AD 654. The Abbot and monks of Ely stole this precious Reliquæ - and translated it to Ely Cathedral where it was interred near her three Royal sisters, A.D. 974.'

EAST ANGLIA'S THREE CROWNS

It may well be that the three sainted daughters of King Annas (or Anna), had some influence in the design and subject content of the (unofficial) Heraldic Arms of East Anglia. On the other hand, if another suggestion concerning the origin of the Arms be accepted, it may have been their father, the King himself, through whom came the source of the design. 'Unofficial' the Arms may be, but 'recognised' they certainly are: the 'Three Crowns' of East Anglia.

Mystery surrounds the design: nowhere can an authentic explanation for the three Golden Crowns, mounted on a background of rich royal blue, be found; but there are many suggestions.

The town of Bury St. Edmunds recognises the close connection of Edmund, King and Martyr, with their town with a profusion of crowned emblems on all its regalia, as well as in its Cathedral; and John Lydgate, the mediæval poet, suggests that the Crowns of Bury symbolise the sainted Monarch's three obvious virtues: Chastity, Kingship and Martyrdom. Guillim, an acknowledged Tudor authority on heraldry, delves much further back in time for his explanation; and suggests that a Celtic King of Ancient Britain named Belinus, who reigned as King of his tribe somewhere about the year 410 B.C., had three crowns because he was Overlord of `Three Countries' at the same time.

The connection between the Arms and the members of King Anna's family is said to be revealed in the heraldry of the Anglican See of Ely; representing the three Abbesses of the Monastery in the Isle who were also queens: Etherreda, wife of the King of Northumberland; Saxburga, Queen of Kent; and Erminalda, each renowned for her holiness.

When Anna fell in the battle near Blythburgh, Jarmin, his son perished with him; but their ally, Cenwaath, King of Wessex, who was engaged in the fight on their side, escaped. Those were blood-thirsty days, three East Anglian kings being killed in two centuries: Anna in 654; Sigebert in 637 and Edmund murdered by the Danes at Hoxne in 870. One theory which seeks to explain the mystery of the Arms is that the Crowns of these three kings were buried to protect them from invaders, and commemorated collectively in pictorial regalia. The Crown of Saint Edmund is usually depicted as being pierced by arrows; signifying his death from archery while bound to a tree. This ending of his life is dramatically portrayed in a mural in the parish church at Pickering in Yorkshire.

It may be that this story of the three buried crowns is true; and that one of them has been recovered. In the final years of the 17th century an ancient silver crown was unearthed at Rendlesham, where Rædwald had a palace. It could have been his, or even one of those said to have been hidden.

Remembering that East Anglia was repeatedly invaded by marauding Scandinavians and Norsemen, it seems to be logical to look for an answer to the problem of the Arms in the influence the visits of these invaders had upon the area. Sweden, in honouring her `Three Crowns' acknowledges them as symbolic representations of three ancient Pagan gods, Odin, Fro and Thor; but in the parish church at Preston, near Lavenham in Suffolk, there are representations of the Crowns of Uffa, King of the Eastern Angles, and of Swen, King of Sweden.

Uffa, the 4th century King of the Angles, appears in that great legendary poem, *Beowulf,* along with his namesake, King Offa of Mercia, who reigned from 757 to 796. The names Uffa, Offa and Oford, or their connotations, are in use in East Anglia today.

Could it be that the 'Three Crowns' of East Anglia take their rise in their connection with the daughters of King Anna, or through the historic Uffa, Swen and Offa who knows?

THE BATTLE OF SOLE BAY

In 1672 the Dutch were preparing a massive assault upon England and, advised that a major attack was imminent, a fleet of English men o' war lay at anchor off Southwold, together with a fleet of their allies, the French. The Duke of York and the Earl of Sandwich were in command of the English vessels and, it being Whitsun, most of the crews were on shore-leave, bringing a roaring trade to the hostelries of the district. All was calm and peaceful as everyone expected it to be until, during the night of the 27th - 28th March, a French frigate sailed in, in haste, with the news that a Dutch fleet was advancing upon the anchored allies.

Crews were hastily re-assembled while, stricken with fear, the French fleet fled, leaving the English to face the enemy alone. The Dutch were commanded by that outstanding Admiral, De Ruyter, a master of tactic and manoeuvre; who caused terrible carnage in a battle in which both sides fought valiantly and neither side really won. Claims and counter-claims were made for both contestants, but in the end neither side could claim the laurels.

In Wake's *Southwold and its Vicinity,* there is a versified description of the Battle of Sole Bay which reads:

>One day as I was sitting still
>Upon this side of Dunwich Hill
>And looking on the ocean,
>By chance I saw De Ruyter's fleet
>With Royal James' squadron meet
>In sooth it was a noble treat
>To see that brave commotion.

I cannot stay to name the names
Of all the ships that fought with James,
Their number or their tonnage:
But this I say; the noble host
Right gallantly did take his post,
And covered all the hollow coast
From Walberswick to Dunwich.

The French, who should have joined the Duke
Full far astern did lag, and look,
Although their hulls were lighter;
But nobly faced the Duke of York,
Though some may wink, and some may talk,
Right stoutly did his vessel stalk
To buffet with De Ruyter.

Well might you hear the guns, I guess,
From Sizewell Gap to Easton Ness,
The show was rare and sightly,
They battled without let or stay
Until the evening of that day;
'Twas then the Dutchman ran away
The Duke had beat them tightly.

Of all the battles gained at sea
This was the rarest victory
Since Philip's grand Armada:
I will not name the rebel, Blake,
He fought for Horson Cromwell's sake;
And yet was forced three days to take
To quell the Dutch bravado.

So now we've seen them take to flight
This way and that; where'ere they might
To windward or to leeward;

Here's to King Charles, and here's to James,
And here's to all the Captain's names;
And here's to all the Suffolk Dames;
And here's to House of Stuart!

Evidence of the type of armament used in the battle came to light three hundred years after the event. The *Daily Telegraph* reported on 7th May, 1976, that "... a cannon, thought to have been on the sea-bed for more than three hundred years has been hauled in by a trawler off Southwold. It is 7½ feet long, and possibly a relic of the Battle of Sole Bay."

In the church of St Andrew at Amptill in Bedfordshire there is a monument to the memory of Richard Nicholls, a sea-faring man, who died in the Battle of Sole Bay. The cannon-ball said to have killed him is embedded in the pediment.

THE SPOOKS OF SOLE BAY

There are thousands of houses in Britain reputed to be haunted. Perhaps the most famous of them all was the former Rectory in the village of Borley, near Sudbury, on the Essex side of the River Stour. Before it was mysteriously destroyed by fire in 1939 the ghosts accredited with being there went berserk, throwing bricks and other things about, scribbling messages on walls, being wafted to and fro both inside and outside the building, and, most ghastly of all, turning wine prepared for Holy Communion into ink. For an account of the ghastly activities read *The most haunted house in England* and *The end of Borley Rectory*, both by Harry Price.

Those who profess to delve into the occult have several theories concerning ghosts; theories which seem to differentiate between poltergeists and spectres. Poltergeists, which are never seen, but throw things about, are not, it is claimed, ghosts at all, but energetic forces emanating from some living person; while another theory is that they are spirits which are independent of living people, but who draw their energy from some person to whom they are attached.

Ghosts are said to be quite insignificant when compared with other manifestations, and in the hundreds of accounts of `sightings' they are of the two kinds most commonly seen. Men of impressive intellectual ability, such as Pliny, Charles Dickens, Arthur Conan Doyle and even the Revd. L John Wesley, believed in ghosts; and in our own age of clinical investigations there is no decline of interest in the subject, in fact the opposite is the case. Whether or not people `believe' in ghosts there is no doubt that the fascination persists.

One of the simplest, yet truest, keys to the understanding of the subject of ghosts is in Charles Dickens' *A Christmas Carol*; in it Scrooge asks the spirit of Jacob Marley, "Why do spirits walk the earth?", to which the phantom replied:

"It is required of every man that the spirit within him should walk abroad among his fellow men, and if that spirit goes not forth in life, it is condemned to do so after death and witness what it cannot share, but might have shared on earth and turned to happiness."

Dickens seems to give this theory of a supernatural presence emphasis when he describes the arrival of the `First of the Three Spirits'. "Scrooge, starting up into a half-recumbent attitude, found himself face to face with the unearthly visitor; as close to it as I am now to you, and I am standing in the spirit at your elbow."

East Anglia is reputed to be particularly prone to ghostly activities. Reference has already been made in these pages to the presence of the Roman Centurion at the Strood, joining Mersea Island to the mainland, and of the Viking warrior on the shore nearby. There are many more. In the northern parts of Norfolk there are the ghosts of Broadland; spirits which are said to annually perpetuate an ancient deed or to revive a rite practised in days gone by. For example; it is said that on certain days between the Ides of March and the Nones of October, there arises, in the centre of Wroxham Broad, a Roman Amphitheatre in which the games and entertainments of the Roman occupying forces were held. Likewise, on the surface of Barton Broad there appears, from time to time, the face of a beautiful girl, who is sound asleep. At Beccles the thirty-first of August is the date for the appearance of three skeletal musicians, playing mediæval instruments.

At Bungay the phenomenon takes the form of a Black Dog, a replica of which can be seen today at the top of a lamp standard by the Butter Cross in the town.

The story goes that on a Sunday morning in the year 1577 a terrific storm burst over the town during the morning church service and the Black Dog, which had been concealed under the Altar, rushed out through the Church and vanished through the door, leaving in its wake several persons dead and a number injured. A plaque in the town records:

All down the Church, in midst of fire
The hellish monster flew;
And passing onwards to the quire
He many people slew.

There are numerous stories of coaches and horses, clanking chains, nocturnal visitations, footsteps, and a headless Anne Boleyn; some of the most interesting centred around Sole Bay.

At Walberswick one hears of spectral appearances in an old railway cutting known locally as Dead Man's Gulley, where, it is said, riders are in danger of losing control of their horses, who shy as though they were aware of something their rider cannot see. The old Anchor Inn, demolished in the 1930s, was said to have an underground passage wherein was found irrefutable evidence of smugglers' occupation. It was also credited with being the habitation of a ghost, but such a story may well have been concocted by the `... handlers of uncustomed goods' in order to deter unwelcome visitors.

The Priory at Blythburgh is another location where animals shun certain parts of the grounds, while the ancient buildings themselves, or what is left of them, echo footsteps which can be heard on the stairs or in a passage which leads to them. The venerable Blythburgh White Hart Inn is another haunted building. Originally it was the Ecclesiastical Court House, associated with the Priory, part of the building dating back to the 13th century.

Sharp knockings on a solid oak door have been described as "... by someone wearing a ring" which may raise conjectures about the Prior who almost certainly wore such an adornment as part of his official insignia. This hostelry is also credited with being a centre for witchcraft, but, as the Inn was also a mecca for the smuggling fraternity this may also have been a guise to keep people away.

Blythburgh's most famous ghost is named Black Toby, who, it is said, can be seen on the road known as Toby Walks to the south of the village. Tobias Gill, a coloured soldier of the Regiment of Dragoons which was stationed at Blythburgh in 1750, was accused of murdering a girl named Ann Blackmore on the Common. He was convicted and sentenced to death, eventually being hung in chains at the cross-roads. It is believed that those who are out very late at night. on the Common may see Toby driving a team of headless horses, searching for a place of repose as, because of the manner of his execution, he had no grave.

Spectral coaches, headless horses and/or riders are reported from a number of places in East Anglia, as also are black dogs.

In Southwold the great story of a ghostly presence is connected with the Battle of Sole Bay. Before the battle the English Fleet was laying at anchor peacefully in the Bay. Under such circumstances the Commanders preferred to sleep ashore and James, Duke of York, and Edmund Montague, Earl of Sandwich, elected to spend the night at a house known as Cammels (now Sutherland House) facing the main street in Southwold.

There was in the house a sixteen year old maid-servant, whose sleeping quarters were on the top floor, but the night the Earl arrived she moved into a large room on the first floor! On the morning when the Naval action was joined on the Bay, the Earl over-slept, and was consequently late arriving on board his Flagship, the *Royal James*, and thus late in entering the Battle. Gunned down by the Dutch, his ship was destroyed, and he was killed. The servant-girl waited in vain for his promised return.

It is said that sometimes she can be seen sitting at a window on the first floor of the house, looking out for him. If this is true, she waits in vain, for the Earl's body was picked out of the sea near Harwich, and eventually buried, with appropriate ceremony, in the North Aisle of the Henry VII Chapel in Westminster Abbey.

Southwold has other ghosts. A local tailor used to talk about footstep in a room over his shop; a headless Gunner is said to stalk on Gun Hill; there is a phantom Lady of Shuck's Hill; the woman in black who emerges from the cliffs; and a strange fisherman carrying a lamp and his catch.

THE EMPORIUM OF HERRING

LOWESTOFT

Lowestoft began when a group of fishermen built a cluster of cottages about the Ness, England's farthest point east. Through the years this small community developed into a valuable fishing port and an attractive holiday resort for those who enjoy fine walks and vigorous sea-breezes. It now has a frontage to the sea almost five miles in length, and is linked with Oulton Broad, which is nearly part of the town.

Quickly developing the fishing industry, Lowestoft had become a port of national importance by the 14th century. In the time of Henry VIII her ships were engaged in cod fishing in Icelandic waters, and herring fishing was the mainstay of the town's economy for generations. Lowestoft has always lived off the sea, but has continually had to fight the sea for its survival. In common with other places on the East Coast, erosion has always presented a real problem. Between 1903 and 1949 three quarters of a million pounds were spent on sea defences, at a time when High Water Mark advanced four hundred yards at the northern end of the Borough.

The Lowestoft Lifeboat Station was founded in 1801, and six

years later the *Frances Ann*, the first life-boat to be equipped with sails, was launched. During her forty-eight years' service she was credited with saving three hundred lives. The Lowestoft lighthouses were the earliest recorded on the shores of England, that on the north side of the town, dating back to 1609. Wood to burn for the light had to be carried up iron steps to maintain the beacon, which must have been a herculean task. All that now remains of that lighthouse is a heap of stones beside the entrance to Belle Vue Park; the modern light, a short distance away, serves today's needs.

The main street of Lowestoft was built parallel with the cliffs, being connected with all other streets by passages or alley-ways known as 'Scores', a description presumably adopted because they closely resembled gashes in the cliff-face called by that name. Above the dunes were built the curing-houses for smoking the herring, and wooden frames for drying the fishing nets.

The town began to acquire its modern character in 1847 with the coming of the railway, which made it possible for the fish, landed at the newly-constructed harbour, to be transported more quickly to the London markets. Gradually other industries settled in the town: shipbuilding became an important source of revenue, as did the coach-building works.

One industry, now defunct, which flourished for a time was the manufacture of porcelain. In 1756, Hewling Luson, of Gunton, discovered extensive clay formations on his estate, and opened a porcelain factory. Decorated with views of Lowestoft, or with simple Chinese landscapes, the products were manufactured in large numbers, but their popularity did not last for long, and in 1803 the factory was closed. A range of characteristic specimens of this work may be seen in the museum at Norwich Castle.

At the same time as its industrial development, Lowestoft's South Town began to grow up as a holiday resort, with large hotels and all types of accommodation.

The mediæval parish church dominating the town, is a noble building, with a nave attached to a tower and spire of earlier date. It has an excellent pier-arcade, and a roof run right through from east to west without a break.

The story of Lowestoft's past would not be complete without reference to its involvement in smuggling. Somewhat more sophisticated than elsewhere, the `runners' at Lowestoft used the harbour and its shipping for their ventures, as one story will illustrate.

Legend claims that the Rector was called upon early one morning, to go aboard a ship lying in the harbour to give comfort to a seaman who was said to be dying of fever. Because of the nature of the illness a hurried funeral was necessary in order that the ship might sail without delay. The contents of the grave did not rest long in peace - the casket was disinterred later in the morning and found to contain a profitable consignment of Continental lace.

Two famous sons of Lowestoft were Thomas Nash (1567 - 1601) and Benjamin Britten. Nash, a rabelaisian poet, took a gloomy view of his native town, saying that he preferred Yarmouth "... because I have money lent me (there)". Britten, son of a local dentist, became home-sick while in America and returned to a group of saltings which he owned at Snape and there founded the musical environment which has grown to what it is now the Aldeburgh Festival.

NORFOLK

THE TOWN ACROSS THE BOUNDARY

GREAT YARMOUTH

When Roman soldiers garrisoned the East Anglian coastline only
a sand-bank existed where the town of Great Yarmouth now
stands. The Romans had their town at Caister, to the north, and
their great naval base and fort at Burgh Castle to the south, and
nothing much between. The coming of the Saxons saw a few huts
spring up on the sand-bank, presumably for their fishermen, and
from that small beginning the development expanded. In Norman
times fishermen from the south coast, particularly from Dover
and Rye became aware of the seasonal herring shoals and came
annually for the `Herring Voyage'. As time went on visitors from
distant places came to buy the herrings, and it became necessary
for Edward the Confessor to regulate proceedings by appointing
a Controller of the Herring Fair. This he did by designating the
Bailiffs of the Cinque Ports to that office, an arrangement which
continued until the 17th century, when it lapsed.

The name of Yarmouth became synonymous with herrings.
The passing of the Statute of Herrings in 1357 fixed a maximum
price for the fish, regulated the measurement of quantity by ruling
that a `Hundred' was six score, and a `Last' numbered ten
thousand. Further, to avoid crews selling their catch before
reaching harbour, the Statute made it compulsory for the boats to
be docked before such transaction could take place; thus retaining
monopoly for the Yarmouth traders.

Yarmouth suffered great financial difficulties in the 16th
century through the expense of trying to keep the harbour mouth
open from the shifting sand, and also attempting to keep the
River Yare on its route to the sea.

It is a long, narrow town, built on a spit of land threatened by
water. It has no option as to its shape because the river flowing

behind the town precludes any development in depth, and any expansion has to be lengthwise from south to north. There has always been a struggle with the Rivers Waveney, Bure and Yare, each having, at one time, had a separate exit to the North Sea. For many years the people of Yarmouth attempted to unite the rivers into a single estuary, but without success, until in 1567 Joast Johnson, a Dutchman, began work on a project which eventually was successful. When it is realised that the river which still flows on the same course today is the water-shed of Broads and the Waveney Valley, it is easy to understand why the discharge of such a work on the rivers which placed Yarmouth in financial straits; they had to sell the church plate, the church bells and some of the vestments to raise money to meet their obligations. Further financial embarrassment was caused by competition from Dutch fishermen. These either sailed into Yarmouth and sold their catch at a lower price than the local fishermen, or they went to a Continental port and sold, thus undermining the Yarmouth men's export trade. After a long struggle and strong protests, an Act of Parliament finally drove the Dutchmen from British waters; and Yarmouth celebrated: but not for long! Instead of the boats from the Low Countries, the Scottish luggers came instead. Every year a large fleet sailed from the North, until in the First World War it was not unusual for a thousand boats to be fishing for Yarmouth herrings. The Herring Drifters were probably the most important of all the vessels to enter the port of Yarmouth, each accompanied by a flock of screeching gulls. The hardy crews of these tight little vessels risked their lives to provide fish for what had become a major industry of curing the fish. Herring swim in shoals, and by laying up to one hundred nets each, cabled together, the Drifters, beating up against the tide, were able to bring in enough fish to keep the thousand or so Scottish fisher-girls, who had come south with their boats, busy gutting, cleaning, curing and then packing the fish for sale.

An old Folk Song, often sung by the girls as they worked, contains this verse:

105

The Pleasure Beach, Great Yarmouth

Burgh Castle

It was a fine and pleasant day
Out of Yarmouth I was faring,
As a cabin boy on a fishing lugger,
To hunt the bonnie shoals of herring.

In the peak days of the industry the drifters tied up at the quays of Yarmouth so close alongside each other that a man could walk across the harbour by stepping from one vessel to the next. Actual proof that this was so is contained in Defoe's remarkable book, *A Tour through the Whole Island of Great Britain by a Gentleman*, which he compiled between 1724 and 1727. He wrote:

Yarmouth is an antient town... plac'd on a peninsular between the River Yare and the sea; and two last lying parallel to one another, and the town in the middle. The River lies on the west side of the town and being grown very large and deep, by a conflux of all the rivers on this side of the country, forms the haven; and the town facing to the west also, and open to the River, makes the finest key (*sic*) in England.

The ships ride here so close, and as it were, keeping up one another, with their head-fasts on shore, that for half a mile together, they go across the stream with their bowsprits over the land, their bowes or heads touching the very warf, so that one may walk from ship to ship as on a floating bridge, all along the shore side.

Sadly, the peak days of the Yarmouth herring industry have now gone; and it seems certain that they will never return.

There was a time when a seaside holiday resort was judged by the size of its beach and its facilities for sea-bathing. Today, however, fun fairs and amusements take precedence over sand and water; but in each connection Great Yarmouth is well endowed to offer whatever is required.

The sea is there, the beach, gay with holiday-makers, fancy hats and wind-breaks, is there; and ice cream and blaring 'music' is there also.

It is difficult, in the height of the summer season to realise that Yarmouth is also a busy and important industrial centre. By the side of the Playground lies the port, noted for its trade in timber which is brought in from the Baltic States and distributed far and wide. Abreast with modern requirements, since the installation of the oil rigs in the North Sea Yarmouth has become particularly busy as a supply base and service depôt for the liberty boats and all manner of other craft which make continuous contact between the rigs and the shore.

The fascination of Yarmouth goes back a long time. Dickens' David Copperfield was intrigued with it, and the inland town of Blundiston was made famous by Dickens when he used it as the place of Copperfield's birth: it was from there that Barkis drove his carrier's cart to Yarmouth. Peggoty's Hut in a upturned boat on the South Denes is there no longer; but a tablet in the town commemorates Dickens' visits. Daniel Defoe was also an admirer, basing the early chapters of *Robinson Crusoe* upon it.

Much of the attractiveness of Yarmouth centres in the `Rows'; a network of thoroughfares in the Old Town which were so narrow the people walking here could touch the walls of the houses on either side of them at the same time. Special narrow carts were constructed to convey merchandise through the Rows; these having the wheels and the shaft ends built in beneath the body. Great destruction in the middle of this old-time town centre was caused by bombing in 1942, but the Rows which survive today are still an attractive shopping area.

The great church, dedicated to St Nicholas, with some Norman work in the Tower, was mostly of 13th century construction. It suffered badly when the Rows were bombed, and was not re-built until 1957-60. The arrangement of the interior resembles that of a cathedral rather that a parish church. Both the choir and the nave house organ consoles and pulpits, and some colourful modern glass give glory to a spectacular building; the largest parish church in England.

In spite of the fact that much of the Old Town was destroyed in the War, and that more has bern torn down to make room for modern building and even despite the slightly tawdry appearance of its sea-front, Great Yarmouth is still worth exploring.

The best epigram with which to conclude this description of Great Yarmouth is a quotation from a work by that indecorous Elizabethan, Thomas Nashe:

Saint Patrike for Ireland: Saint George for England: the Herring for Yarmouth.

THE COAST OF NORFOLK

God drew a map of England
And planted hill and wood,
He looked on stream and heathland
And saw that it was good:
Placed far into a corner
He left a fair domain,
Heath, and Fen and Broadland
Rich pasturage and grain.

When God made Norfolk County
He said they'd love her well,
Who, patient in their wooing
Surrendered to her spell:
So come and visit Norfolk,
Bide till her spell is cast
Then, once you've learned to love her,
You'll love her to the last.

Verses from: *Song of Norfolk* by Canon Frederick C Oakley, Rector of Necton-cum-Holme Hale; 1926 - 1945

THE COASTLINE

Norfolk is wealthy in scenery, history and places of interest. Beside the attractions of the inland scenes, fenland and forest, noble churches and country market towns, the magnificent coastline calls for the attention of all who love unspoilt beauty. As far back as it is possible to trace its history, this coast has witnessed an incessant struggle waged between the land and the sea. This battle still continues, with victories and losses on both sides. There are places where a portion of the cliffs is eaten away by the waves every year. Norfolk has no rock formation in its terrain; with the exception of a short stretch at Hunstanton, the cliffs are composed of boulder-clay which dissolves in the sea-water when attacked by the waves; a fact which accounts for so much of the coast disappearing. There are also parts which have seen the sea retreat, leaving former ports and harbours choked with sand, making access to harbours impossible, with the trading possibilities of towns fading away and their prosperity gone.

This is the Norfolk coastline: nearly a hundred miles of sand-dunes and saltings, of mud-flats, of creeks, cliffs and channels. It has secluded hamlets and busy holiday resorts, nature reserves and promenades. Off-shore there are strong currents of which those who swim must beware; treacherous tides and sand-banks; and the wreck of many a ship lying on the sea-bed. It is one of the most hazardous strips of coast around the British Isles.

For the holiday-maker this is a coast of sandy beaches, of isolated stretches of marsh and flats, with the strong wind and the cry of the birds for company. For the archæologist the coast is rich in history, but for the navigator it is danger all the way, unless he is fully alert,

> The hand that carved Old England's form
> Set Norfolk in the East;
> To catch the sunrise and the storm
> In moods that suit her best
>   *Norfolk*   Ernest Edward Smith

THE GRAVE-YARD OF MANY SHIPS, WINTERTON

Nine miles north of Yarmouth, the village of Winterton lies in quiet seclusion, known hardly at all except for a few holiday-makers and some week-enders who have bought some of the one-time fishermen's cottages. It may not be well known to the land-lubber, but by the seaman it has for centuries been considered the most dangerous part of the East Coast between Tyne and Thames. Winterton owes its reputation as the scene of more ship-wrecks and loss of life than all other parts of the coast put together, to the proximity of the once-dreaded Winterton Ness, a promontory which swept out from the shore to the danger of any vessel failing to give it a wide berth.

Washed and scoured by powerful tides, the Ness has now been swept away, but a map of 1574 shows it in its most dangerous form. To be sure of clearing it, vessels, particularly those sailing out of Yarmouth, were forced to beat a distance out to sea; no easy task in the teeth of a gale and a running tide. Many vessels failed in the attempt and the beaches around Winterton became their graveyard. The wrecks which piled up on the shore witnessed to the tragedy enacted; but the local population was not slow in profiting, not only by appropriating the ship's cargo, but also by making use of the ship's furnishings and timbers. Daniel Defoe visited Winterton in 1722 and wrote:

> There is not a shed, nor a barn, nor a stable, nay, not the pales of the fences or yards, not a hogstye, but was made of planks, beams, and timbers, the wreck of ships and the ruin of merchants' and mariners' fortunes.

The great loss of life which occurred at Winterton is commemorated in the magnificent Parish Church of All Saints. In this remarkable building, where, in a county noted for its tall churches, the Tower is said to be taller than any other "...by a Herring and a half", one part is set aside as a `Fishermen's Chapel'. This is furnished with items which have all been taken from ships which have perished in the sea, or made from timbers

111

Winterton

recovered from wrecks. Ships' timbers have been used to make the Altar and at the Crucifix: fishing nets are used as curtains: a ship's lamp provided illumination and ships' ropes cordon off the Sanctuary.

That is history; but happily the story at Winterton is different today. It seems incredible, but it is true, that whereas in other parts of the Norfolk and Suffolk coasts the land is being eaten away by the tide, here it is being built up

Winterton Dunes form a Nature Reserve extending about two miles from the village to where the former 'Old Hundred' stream, which helped to drain the eastern part of Broadland, entered the sea. These dunes, formed by the action of wind and tide, have grown up in front of an earlier coast-line, and consist of high-ridged sand which is very soft and unstable: to attempt to climb to the ridge top from the shore below is almost impossible. However, tufted marram grass and other vegetation throw down roots to bind the sand together, while more is piled upon it, making the ridges higher every time. From the shore side these ridges make a spectacular sight; the wind-swept walls are smooth, with an almost rock-like appearance: on the landward side they graduate into heath and poorly drained and bog-like in parts One of the noticeable features about this sand is the absence of shells, usually they are found in abundance on East Anglian beaches.

In this low lying area of about two-hundred-and-sixty acres are a number of 'Dune slacks'; water-filled or water-logged hollows, where a variety of plants grow. Here, in an ideal environment, the Natterjack Toad is to be found (the 'Natterjack' is to be distinguished from the common toad by reason of the yellow stripe running down its back). As some of the slacks have dried out a new pool has been purposely built in order that the Natterjack may have a permanent place in which to live and breed.

The adder breeds among the dunes, and, as it is the only poisonous snake in Britain, visitors are warned to take care when walking in the grass. The flight of an occasional kestrel adds interest for the bird-watcher, who may also see warblers, chiffchaffs and many larks in summer, and a variety of resting migratory species in the winter. The most important breeding species in the Reserve is the little tern which nests in a shallow hole in the shingle, just above high-water mark, from April to August. This is one of the principal breeding grounds for this bird in Britain.

HISTORY IN A BUNDLE OF LETTERS

PASTON

Among the of smaller communities lying along the coast to the north of Yarmouth; Sea Palling, Happisburgh, Bacton, Mundsley, Trimmingham and Overstrand, one of the smallest, Paston, is the most important. This tiny hamlet has made a great contribution to the rich literary heritage of England, out of all proportion to its size. A bundle of about a thousand letters written in the 15th century have, since being found, become famous as they furnish a detailed account of the private domestic life of a typical country squire, as it was lived at the time that they were written.

It is a wonder that they have survived; they have been 'lost', disregarded, kept in a drawer in a chemist's shop in Diss and given to a man named John Fenn of Dereham. Fenn proposed to publish a selection of them in 1787, but was discouraged from doing so, and ultimately the whole collection came to light in the British Museum.

The Paston Letters, as they are known, enable those who read them to trace the fortunes of the family whose name they bear, by whom they were written and received, in great detail. They show what the members of the family had to eat, the clothes they wore, how and where those clothes were obtained, the family's financial obligations and difficulties, their business embarrassments, the way in which the adults addressed each other, filial respect, and much more: an altogether illuminating portrayal of their times as can be found anywhere.

Church interior, Paston

Cromer in sea mist

History is made by the inter-actions of people. To try and envisage these people as they were, to follow the course of their lives as they were lived, cannot be done in any better way than by studying the correspondence between responsible members of a household. Family letters reveal life as it was lived from within s how the actors on the stage of life react to given circumstances; how they and their environment influenced each other; what hopes and fears trembled within their breasts; and what were the repercussions and achievements or failures. *The Paston Letters* tell us all these things; and at the same time the letters which they received from Bishops and servants, from Dukes or men in prison, from priests and rude parishioners, all help in constructing a picture of the life and social circumstances of their times.

One other link with the 15th century in this hamlet is the fine old Tithe Barn standing by the roadside. With its great length of 163 feet, its steep thatched roof, and alternating tie-beams and hammer beams, it is a remaining connection with the Paston family who lived at the Hall, of which nothing now remains. Beside the Barn stands the Parish Church, also thatched; here the family worshipped and here are a number of their tombs.

Norfolk is a county beautified by a large number of village signs, most of them the work of local craftsmen who employed their skill in portraying the salient features of the history or trade of their community. Paston is no exception: the importance of the Letters is perpetuated in their sign which shows an ink bottle, a quill pen and a parchment roll.

CROMER FOR CRABS

Cromer describes itself as 'The Gem of the Norfolk Coast', a description which befits one of the East Coast's most famous holiday resorts to which thousands of holiday-makers travel annually. It is not a 'picture-postcard' resort, where beds of brilliantly coloured flowers reach down to meet the sands; there are flowers, but they are on the top of the cliffs; Cromer meets the sea with stone and concrete, looking like some mighty fortress; because in the past it has suffered mightily from the attacks of the North Sea waves.

At one time Cromer was not next to the sea; the village stood inland, with another named Shipden between it and the water's edge: but this is the spot on "...the bulge of Norfolk" where the hungry waves and scouring currents, rushing down from the North, first bite into the land. Shipden has been engulfed and, like other places, has disappeared for ever. So Cromer became a seaside community; and the population were obliged to devise means by which to save their town; hence the concrete!

The glory of Cromer is its Lifeboat; and her most famous son is a man who was a member of the Lifeboat's Crew for fifty eight years. Twelve miles out to sea from Cromer Pier lie the notorious Haisborough Sands which have taken a heavier toll on shipping than any other sandbank around the coast, with the possible exception of the Goodwins. Principally because of the presence of these disaster-making sands it is imperative that a Lifeboat should always be on station at Cromer: some of the ugliest sea-dramas have been enacted on these sands, and the Cromer Boat has a proud record of service in life-saving.

For fifty-eight years a member of the Lifeboat crew, and Coxswain for most of that time, Henry Blogg has passed into history as a legend. His exploits have never been forgotten. This remarkable man once drove his Lifeboat clean on to the deck of the stricken *Selapoy* to snatch two near-lifeless sailors out of the rigging: on another occasion he chased the *Porthcawl*, laden with esparto grass and blazing like a torch, all the way to the Yarmouth Roads before he could come alongside the red-hot hull. Henry Blogg was awarded the Royal National Lifeboat Institution's Gold Medal for Gallantry three times and its Silver Medal four times. He died in 1954, aged 78, and a memorial was erected outside the Council Offices in Cromer in his memory. The bronze bust, showing him in Lifeboat uniform, looks with unseeing eyes toward the Pier where stands the Boat-house and slipway from where he

Cromer church

left on his mercy missions on so many occasions. A Tribute on the pedestal reads: "One of the bravest men that ever lived".

An outstanding feature of Cromer is the massive Tower of the fine Perpendicular parish church, rising to a height of one-hundred-and-sixty feet. This served as a lighthouse in the days before the purpose-built lighthouse tower was built on the cliffs towards Overstrand. The method of illumination when the church tower was used was for a lamp to be hung in a window, a square hole contrived in the wall of the Tower. Nowhere in Cromer can one escape this Tower; on the roads leading into the town; the beach or the streets; its presence commands attention; making everything else appear diminutive beside it. The western porch of the church, with its mediæval niches and battlements is probably the oldest part of the building because most of the Church was re-built after demolition of the 13th century church standing on the same site. The windows were filled with richly coloured glass in the Victorian Age, featuring figures from the Old Testament and Saint Paul preaching on Mars Hill. The streets radiating from Church Square are very narrow and winding, a paradise for the antiquarian, but frustrating for the modern motorist.

Cromer is famous for its crabs which, together with those obtainable in nearby Sheringham, which come from the same source, are rated the best in England. The little boats with which the crabs are caught are unique: very small, double ended, clinker built, with a great beam and very full bilges. Lightly constructed, they have numerous but very light ribs to the frame, eminently suitable for beach-handling as they have to be.

At rare intervals when the tide is exceptionally low, traces of the past, in the shape of stumps of trees which stood in a long-submerged forest are exposed to view; while on the beach fossilised remains of prehistoric monsters have been found. It was in the not-so-far distant 18th century that the town began to take the form of a fashionable seaside resort. Since then it has gone ahead, adapting itself, within its self-prescribed limits, to the changing needs of succeeding generations.

BEACH PEBBLES AND THREE LIFEBOATS

Sheringham lies in a deep declivity in the cliffs and has transformed itself from an old-fashioned fishing village, with quaint
cottages and timbered boat-houses tucked away in narrow streets,
into one of the principal eesorts on the Norfolk coast. Surviving
parts of the original village can still be seen, with crab pots and
fishing nets deposited in odd corners among pebble-faced cottages
of another age. The beach has provided the pebbles used in this
unique form of building. Piled up in large layers along the shore,
the pebbles serve Sheringham well as bulwarks against the
encroaching tide; and have been used for facing walls in a number
of other villages along this coast. The smaller and most uniform
pebbles were generally used for the walls at the front of the
buildings, while less prominent elevations were dressed with larger
stones. In this style of building the pebbles were used whole as
distinct from the more general flint flush-work, where the stones
were napped and used with the newly exposed surface outside.

As the years passed and the population increased, the income
derived from holiday-makers far exceeded that earned from the
more hazardous and less lucrative fishing, until catering for
visitors became the mainstay of the town's economy.

Sheringham's first Lifeboat was stationed in the town in 1839,
a private venture by the Hon. Mrs. Upcher: The Royal Naval Lifeboat Institution took over the responsibility for its maintenance
in 1867, since when the boats and crews of the Sheringham boat
have been instrumental in saving a great number of lives.

One famous rescue by the Sheringham boat is commemorated
in a unique fashion in the bar of an ancient hostelry standing
practically on the water's edge. The Two Lifeboats Hotel began life
as an inn about 1720, when it was the centre of the social life of
the community. Called the New Inn it was closed in the early
1800s as "... a place of bad repute". Re-opened later, it established
a good reputation, and developed into a prosperous and pleasing
seaside hotel. In the bar is a remarkable wrought-iron screen, with

Sheringham cliffs

Weybourne Church and Priory

an explanation which reads:

"Made for his City and Guilds examination by an apprentice blacksmith; Alan Todd" the artistic work shows

"The Two Lifeboats" - *Augusta* and *Duncan* - rescuing the crew of eight from the wreck of the Norwegian Brig *Caroline* at Spallow Gap, Sheringham, on December 6th, 1882."

Today the amusement arcades in the main street contrast strangely with the quiet simplicity of former days: ancient and modern are well jumbled together in Sheringham.

ANOTHER INVASION SITE?

The undulating countryside hereabouts gives the impression of slight hills and valleys, and is known as the East Anglian Heights. This is part of a range running parallel with the coastline, and is called locally the Holt to Cromer Ridge, as it extends between these two towns. It is a wooded area of fir and birch trees, with bracken and heather making a carpet beneath.

In a hollow at the foot of this higher ground lies Weybourne, with its church tower constituting a landmark between open fields and the sea. Beside the church stands the ruined tower of the 13th century Priory, a monastic House of the Canons Regular of Saint Augustine. Together, Church and Priory ruins make one of the most interesting of the smaller monastic sites in Norfolk.

The Augustine or Austin Canons, who lived according to a Rule drawn up by Saint Augustine, Bishop Hippo in North Africa in the 5th century, was an Order which existed in the mediæval church placed between the monk and the secular priest. They lived as a community subject to monastic regulations and were free to serve churches in the district as Parish Priests when the need arose, particularly those parishes fro which the Priory received tithes or endowments.

Weybourne Priory was founded in 1200 as a dependant cell of the much larger Augustinian House at West Acre, which had been established earlier by Ralph de Toeni, whose family were hereditary Standard Bearers to the Duchy of Normandy. The Priory was endowed with the Church and Manor of Weybourne, but its possessions were never extensive, and throughout the whole of its history it was nearly always understaffed as well as being in financial difficulties. When Bishop Goldwell of Norwich conducted a Visitation of the Priory in 1494, the community consisted of the Prior and three Canons: twenty years later there was only one Canon, and so it remained until in the end "... the poverty of the House made it impossible to support even this small number."

At the Dissolution the buildings and other properties were granted to Sir John Gresham, the founder of the famous school in Holt which bears his name. From him, it eventually passed into the hands of the Walpole family, patrons of the living connected with the Parish Church.

The actual shore-line at Weybourne is dramatically different from that in other parts of Norfolk. Whereas in many places coastal marshland separates the shore from the developed areas, here the higher ground meets the sea with nothing between. In place of dunes and marshes there are cliffs, sometimes one hundred feet deep, rising to three times that height before dying away again into marshland some miles in the distance.

From time to time when invasion has been a real threat to England it has been rumoured that such an event was to take place on this part of the coast. Landing parties require deep water to bring their vessels inshore: here at Weybourne, in less than six paces from the water's edge, the water is too deep for a man to stand. It was here that Napoleon planned to invade England, and it is suggested in Erskine Childers' *The Riddle of the Sands* that Germany was planning an invasion at the same spot in 1912, using barges from the Elbe.

No armed invasion has been successfully accomplished on this coast since the time of the Danes; but the fear that there might be an attempt to do so has lasted throughout the centuries.

HARBOURS THAT ARE NO MORE

CLEY-NEXT-THE-SEA

The great days of this quaint little town (with a name correctly pronounced to rhyme with `sky') are gone, but it is still delightfully picturesque, with old houses and the most famous of Norfolk's many windmills. Cley Mill has probably been the subject of more photographs and artists' paintings than any other mill in the county.

The town's history goes back over three thousand years. Barrows on the heather-covered uplands stir the imagination with thoughts of ancestors hundreds of years ago; but the most important part of its history was fashioned when it was a wealthy seaport, with Flemish wool merchants a familiar sight in its streets. There is still an atmosphere reminiscent of their presence in the town, with evidence of Dutch influence in some of its architecture. Prosperity vanished, however, when, in common with other towns along this coast, Cley Harbour was silted up and sea-going vessels could anchor at its quays no more.

Before this happened the estuary of the River Glaven broadened to form an extensive harbour from which Cley merchants conducted a thriving export trade during the boom years of the East Anglian woollen industry. Today the Glaven, although picturesque, is in places not much more than a stream.

Rising in a quiet valley known to the Saxons whose settlement was in the heart of a forest, the river runs through the village of Letheringsett, where it turns the mighty wheel of the water mill, still in action at certain times today. In this village the 12th century church was built by Hamon Grimbaldus, renowned as `Grimbaldus Medicus', physician to King Henry I. Cedars, oaks and other trees, survivors or descendants of the original forest, surround the village and shade the grave of Johnson Jix, the village blacksmith of Longfellow's day. By supreme effort Jix educated himself in science; an inscription in his memory recording that "...

He advanced from the forge to the crucible, and from the horse-shoe to the chronometer".

About half-way along the road running from Letheringset to Cley, astride the Glaven as it runs through its wooded valley to the sea, lies the delightful little village of Glanford. The church is set in a garden on a hill; an old church, once dilapidated and in decay, but beautifully restored by Sir Alfred Jodrell as a memorial to Adela, his wife who died in 1896. A constant benefactor to the village, Sir Alfred lived at Bayfield House nearby.

Another gift to the village from this generous squire was the Shell Museum, housed in a small building with Dutch gables, built by the employees of Sir Alfred who worked on the Bayfield estate. It houses a collection of shells which Sir Alfred had collected from many parts of the world. There are shells of every hue, shells delicately coloured and shells in unusual shapes and sizes. The exhibition also contains lovely jewels, historic accoutrements, specimens of agate ware and much more beside.

One of the church towers which can be seen from Cley is that of Wivton, a mile away. Once one of the Glaven-side sea-ports, (Cley, Wivton and Blakeney) Wivton shared with the other two the estuary of the river, but now it is an inland village. Denuded of its importance but jealous of its history, Wivton is conspicuous because of its church with a majestic tower. The builders of this 15th century edifice gave it splendid arcades, a clerestoried nave and a richly carved font. The latter is now, unfortunately, much mutilated by wear an age.

All signs of the former importance of Wivton have disappeared, "Forgotten as a dream dies at the opening day", but the story of one man lives on. James Hackman, after a military career, took Holy Orders and was appointed Rector in 1799. Earlier he had fallen in love with a stay-maker's daughter named Martha Ray, whom he had met at Tinchinbrooke, the ancestral home of the Cromwells at Huntingdon. Martha, who had already given birth to several children fathered by the 4th Earl of Sandwich, resented his attentions and rebuffed his advances. Hackman's passions flared, and five weeks after his installation to the living at Wivton he went to London where, as Martha Ray was leaving Covent Garden Theatre, he shot her dead. His suicide attempt was thwarted, and he was hanged at Tyburn twelve days later.

BLAKENEY

The first documentary reference to Blakeney is in Domesday Book, but evidence of earlier inhabitants are in the Neolithic and Roman artifacts discovered in the district. Also it must be presumed that an estuary as good as the Glaven was then would not be ignored by the Vikings during their raids on the surrounding countryside.

The names by which Blakeney has been identified are of great interest. The earliest name was 'Esnuterle'; then 'Snitterly'; to be followed later by 'Blakeney-alias-Snitterly'; and eventually just Blakeney. Esnuterle and Snitterly occur in Domesday; Blakeneye or Blakene are used in the 13th century, and in 1368 the visitation of the Bishop of Norwich the name of the parish is 'Snyterlie-alias-Blakeney'. There are other instances in Domesday where words similar to 'Sniterley' are used to denote villages situated upon exposed ridges of land. The reason is quite clear: the Old English word 'sniterene' means 'to snow', or when rendered as 'snitter' it can mean 'a biting blast'.

It has been suggested that Blakeney and Snitterly were two separate places, the latter being on an exposed 'ridge' which has since fallen into the sea, but whether or not this is so is unknown; what is known is that 'Snitterly' was granted a market by King Henry III in 1223, and in 1358 a Statute was passed controlling the sale of fish "... in the same towne". It would appear that, whatever they had been before, by the 15th century 'Blakeney' and 'Snitterly' were one and the same place.

In 1296 Maud de Roos founded a Carmelite Friary at Blakeney. The Carmelites were so-called because their origins were connected with Mount Carmel in the Holy Land. In England they were known as 'White Friars' to distinguish them from the

'Black' Dominicans and the 'Grey' Franciscans. Usually the Carmelites preferred to be cloistered near to large towns, so it van be presumed that Blakeney was particularly prosperous at that time, or that they had been assured of support. The Friary grew and prospered until it was disbanded at the Dissolution in 1538, even although Henry VIII had granted a Charter to "...the Guild of Blakeney" to supply fish to "... Monastic Orders" only twenty-three years earlier.

Fishing and the associated trades of Blakeney harbour afforded a convenient cover for piracy and smuggling, which were both extensively practised. Marauding parties were known to board and rob ships sheltering from the great gales that blew across the harbour and on more than one occasion ships outward bound were wrecked off Stiffkey and their cargoes of wool and cloth taken. An example of such a happening is revealed in a report that in 1286 Henry Flyk and Hildebrand de Lubeck brought an action against Thomas Borgeys "... for seizing and taking by force a ship laden with cloth that was driven ashore at Blakeney "

It was the Flemish wool merchants who really brought wealth to Blakeney. In common with the neighbouring small ports it was no more unusual to see them on the quayside than it is to see holiday-makers today. But the downfall of the harbour and therefore of the town of Blakeney itself was the work of nature. The sea piled up silt, sand and pebbles to form an off-shore barrier, blocking the harbour mouth.

Through the years this ridge developed and became covered with wild plant-life; migratory birds discovered its rich food store and quickly adopted the area as a 'staging post' on their journeys to and from the tropics or the far north. When the National Trust assumed responsibility for Blakeney Point the permanence and maintenance of the area was assured.

On rising ground behind the village stands Blakeney's proudest possession, the parish church, with the main altar dedicated, as in so many seaside churches, to Saint Nicholas, the Patron Saint of seafarers. The fine west tower rises one hundred feet, and a slender tower on the north-east corner of the church was erected to hold and shine a light as a beacon for sailors in the days before lighthouses.

Blakeney has had associations with three famous Admirals. Sir Christopher Myngs was born in 1625, Myngs entered the service of the navy at a time when there were many fights with the Dutch. According to Pepys, Myngs was "... A man fearing the Lord, of sound principles and blameless life, one of much valour". At the time of the Restoration he was made an Admiral of the Fleet, and because of his vigilance it was almost impossible for anything attempting to sail up the English Channel to escape the attention of his frigates. Myngs was mortally wounded at the Battle of North Foreland in 1666.

Next among the famous trio was Sir John Narborough who, with Myngs, took part in a naval battle off Lowestoft. After his death in 1688 his second wife married the final one of the three, Sir Cloudsley Shovell, who gained distinction at the Battle of Bantry Bay in 1689, and commanded the seige of Toulon in 1707.

Blakeney's real connection with the sea ended when its last sea-going vessel was sold in 1916; after which the town had to fashion a new way of life through being deprived of its shipping and trade.

WELLS-NEXT-THE-SEA

Wells-next-the-Sea has a waterfront lined with quite imposing buildings from which narrow streets climb up from the quayside to the town. Like its neighbours along this coast the great days of the port are gone, the building-up of the sand-bars bringing disaster to its trade. Instead of lapping the quayside with every in-coming tide, the waves lie away in the distance behind a belt of trees, only very quiet waters rise between the banks of a narrow channel to indicate that the tide is in. Occasionally, when the tides are suitable, and this channel is deep enough, a small coasting vessel will cautiously find its way to the quay to unload phosphates and take on a cargo of grain. But these warehouses, this wharf with its massive timber piling, these berths, were not built for the benefit of an occasional tramp steamer; they have seen better days, when larger ships jostled for positions along the water-front, and a regular service was run to the Dutch ports.

The hallmarks of a former prosperity accentuate the great loss which the retiring sea has meant to the one-time flourishing port. However, all connections with maritime activities were not lost: today local fishermen sail out in search of mackerel and shell-fish, while enterprising business people have developed an appeal to holiday-makers, attracting them to the town, and a stretch of sandy beach beyond the pine trees has been brought up to date as a holiday lido for the town's ever-welcome visitors.

COKE OF NORFOLK

At Holkham Hall there lived a man who is credited with turning a wilderness into a fertile and productive garden. He was Thomas William Coke, known as Coke of Norfolk, sometimes styled 'The Father of English Agriculture'.

The founder of the Coke family fortunes was Edward Coke, who lived from 1552 to 1634: the son of a London barrister, who became Sir Edward, Member of Parliament and Lord Chief Justice to King James I. Although he is renowned for his harshness at the trials of the Earl of Essex, Sir Walter Raleigh and Guy Fawkes, he is also remembered as the one who first stood against the King for the Rights of Parliament and the ordinary citizen.

Five generations later, another Thomas Coke (1697 - 1759) built the great mansion known as Holkham Hall in 1734. Ten years later he was created Earl of Leicester, but on his death the title died with him as there was no direct heir. The estate passed to a nephew by marriage Wenham Roberts, who changed his name to Coke, and it was his son, Thomas William Coke, who eventually inherited the estate and later became Earl of Leicester (of the second creation). Thomas William Coke inherited land which was barren, where sheep were half starved, and where it was said that "... two rabbits would fight over one blade of grass".

By continual experimentation with the treatment of the soil and an entirely new system of rotation of the crops he transformed the estate into one which became rich and prosperous, thus giving agriculture a lead in revolutionary practices which have become standard today.

The church in Holkham Park has connections with Saxon times. It will be remembered that one of the daughters of King Anna of the East Anglia was Withburga, some-time Abbess of East Dereham. In her memory the church at Holkham is dedicated to St Withburga; unique in England to have this Saint as its patron.

At the back of Holkham Hall stands the Stable Block, erected about one hundred years after the main building; large enough to house forty horses and a number of carriages. These buildings have now been put to a new use: to hold, on permanent display, a unique collection of bygones.

Dick Joyce, the son of a tenant farmer, began collecting old farm implements when he was a lad; and when his parent's farm carts and other tools were of no further use on the land the boy asked for and was granted permission to store them as objects of an earlier day's work. Gradually the collection increased, until it amounted to several thousand items, large and small; and a home had to be found for them. This was arranged in the Stable Block at Holkham, and there they may be seen today, a fine portrayal of the life of yesterday.

VILLAGES NELSON KNEW

BRANCASTER

The stretch of coastline beyond Holkham is probably the most unspoiled of any in Norfolk; with miles of spacious beaches and acres of rolling dunes. In the whole of East Anglia there are no beaches broader, no scenery wilder and no surroundings more relaxed than along this northern Norfolk seaboard.

Such is the beach at Brancaster where sea, sand and sky merge into one on the horizon, and where wind drives the sand in clouds before it and sways the marram grass until it resembles the movement of the waves

The name 'Brancaster' speaks of Roman occupation. As one of the northernmost garrisons of the Saxon Shore fortifications it housed a unit of Roman cavalry which was supplied and reinforced through the Staithe nearby.

Staithe is the old word for 'landing place'; today not many arrive here, but every year hundreds of people depart for and return from the Island of Scolt Head, one of the best known Bird Sanctuaries in the care of the National Trust. On Scolt Head visitors may see a great variety of birds; some permanent residents and many migratory species; some of this feathered fraternity coming to nest and breed and some as birds of passage, using the island as a dormitory on their way to other parts of the world. Every evening, as dusk falls, skeins of wild-fowl fly in to the island after spending the day feeding on the marshes and in the Fens.

HOLME NEXT-THE SEA and TITCHWELL

The road along the coastline runs through Holme-next-the-Sea and Titchwell. The hamlet of Titchwell gathers around a quaint-looking church, its round tower crowned with a slender spire entirely out of keeping with the rest of the building. On a grass-covered mound in the centre of the cross-roads stands an ancient stone column, originally a signpost pointing pilgrims on their way either along the Peddar's Way or to the Shrine at Walsingham.

The Icknield Way, the chalk ridge which acted as a road for prehistoric travellers who dared to venture into the forests and fens of East Anglia, terminates at Holme, as does Peddar's Way, famous since the Romans built it to connect their garrisons. Cæsar's soldiers constructed Peddar's Way after Boadicea's rising to give themselves greater freedom of movement should such a revolt be attempted again. It was also their plan for mobility to counter trouble in any area of eastern England, for which purpose they also ran a ferry service across the Wash to Lincolnshire. At Thornham they built a Signal Station to warn the Lincolnshire garrison of any trouble among the Iceni on their side of the water.

THE BURNHAMS

A mile or two inland is what has become a prime tourist country, embracing the five Burnham villages. The most important is Burnham Market, the street market after which the village is named being an attraction for residents and visitors alike. Next in importance is Burnham Thorpe, this being the birth-place of Admiral Lord Nelson. Burnham Deepdale has a Saxon Church with a round tower which is only a little higher than the roof of the nave, and consequently presents a stunted appearance. At Burnham Norton the few residents live near a sandy estuary, and at Burnham Overy the cottages line the route to Overy Staithe where small ships can come in from the sea.

THE EAST COAST WHICH FACES WEST

HUNSTANTON

New Hunstanton, the seaside resort, came into being during the Victorian era, when it was developed specifically to cater for the new fashion of spending a holiday by the seaside. Old Hunstanton, a village of quiet lanes, old cottages, a village pond and a fine ancient church, surrounds the great House built by the Le Strange family who did so much to aid the village and its church. It is said that this house has been the Le Strange family home since one of them married a Saxon Lady; certainly Sir Hamon Le Strange built the first part on his return from Crécy; building continued through the years; Sir Roage Le Strange erected the central brick gatehouse in 1500; the archway of the forecourt was designed by Inigo Jones in 1618 and an odd-looking building, erected specially for a head of the family to use when practising his viol, was built in the 17th century.

New Hunstanton is entirely different:: it is now a Mecca for day-trippers, with slot machines, bingo halls and fairgrounds. This was not always so. As the town first found favour with those seeking relaxation it attracted well-to-do elderly people who wanted peace and quiet, in fact it was regarded as being snobbish in the extreme: but all this changed after the Second World War. Recovering from military occupation, Hunstanton set about attracting an entirely new and different class and kind of visitor, and succeeded! Many of those who go to the town arrive in coaches from the Fens, the Midlands and nearby towns in Cambridgeshire. By the sea for the day, the visitors hasten to sample what there is on offer on a front two miles long, with flat beaches where, when the tide recedes a great distance, the water in-shore remains shallow, providing ideal conditions for bathing.

Hunstanton is unique among East Anglian coastal resorts, in that all the other larger towns existed originally as fishing villages, gradually developing in size and attractiveness as their popularity with the public increased. New Hunstanton grew up around a grassy slope which today is the central feature of the town.

There are two other notable features of Hunstanton. One is the sudden rising of a line of cliffs at the end of the Promenade; not ordinary cliffs, but bluffs unique in England and of great interest to geologists. The base consists of a narrow seam of carstone, above which are two distinct layers of chalk, the upper being pure white, the lower terra-cotta pink.

The second feature of considerable attractiveness is occasioned by the town's geographical position: it has the unusual distinction of being an East Coast resort which faces west. This is true of the remainder of the shore of Norfolk from this point to King's Lynn.

Standing on the shore of the Wash, Hunstanton faces the most beautiful sunsets in Britain, because of which on many a Summer evening the holiday crowds come to a halt in their

133

perambulations as the setting sun makes the sea crimson and the cliffs turn to a burnished gold.

One section of Hunstanton's cliffs is known as Saint Edmund's Point. On Christmas Day, 853, into the Wash sailed a fleet of ships, one of which carried a youth of fifteen, who landed at this point of the Norfolk coast. He was named Edmund, and had been brought from Germany to be crowned King of the Eastern Angles in succession to Offa who had died. His subsequent history is sad: his Coronation took place at Bures one year later - on Christmas Day, 854; his reign was short and tormented and he was executed by Danish invaders at Hoxne. About the year 1216 a chapel, the scant remains of which can still be seen, was built on the cliff-top to commemorate Edmund's landing. There pilgrims passing on their way to the Shrine at Walsingham, paused to offer prayers and to partake of the supposedly curative waters at Hunstanton's healing springs. The ruins of the chapel are now dedicated as a memorial to the men and women of East Anglia who lost their lives in the world wars.

Nearby stands the white tower of the Hunstanton Lighthouse which ceased to be used for the purpose for which it was erected many years ago.

ISABELLA'S PRISON

Deserted by the sea which once lapped its quaysides but is now two miles away, the cluster of red-roofed cottages at Castle Rising are but a poor reminder of the glories of the past. Once important, Castle Rising as a port had a Mayor ranking of some importance in the County of Norfolk, but the sea withdrew, dealing the town a blow from which it never recovered.

Two thousand years of history are embodied in this place: Roman legions built massive earth-works one thousand feet in circumference, to surround their encampment, and the Norman, William de Albini, who married the widow of King Henry I and became Earl of Sussex, raised the great castle and the church

Castle Rising; Keep from gateway

nearby. The particularly well-preserved castle stands within the depression made by the earthworks, and visitors may pass through the doorways, climb the stairs and enter rooms where that history has been enacted.

After the death of Mortimer Queen Isabella, who had connived at the death of Edward II, was imprisoned in this Castle for nearly thirty years during which time she, no doubt, looked longingly at the sea which almost lapped the wall beneath the window of the room which was her prison. In spite of receiving visits from her son, Edward III, no remission was granted to her, and after entering the Castle as a young woman she stayed until she was old.

Not far from Castle Rising is the historic town of King's Lynn:

> Rising was a seaport town
> When Lynn was but a marsh;
> Now Lynn it is the sea-port,
> And Rising fares the worse.

KING'S LYNN

The River Great Ouse rises in Northamptonshire at Steane, about three miles from Brackley; it skirts a mile or so of the Oxfordshire border then passes through Buckinghamshire, Bedfordshire, Huntingdon, Cambridgeshire and the Isle of Ely, to enter Norfolk and empty itself in the Wash. It could be said that in part it constitutes the Western natural water-border of East Anglia, particularly when its various tributaries are taken into consideration. These tributaries add Suffolk, Essex and Hertfordshire to the impressive list of counties through which it flows. It is the fifth longest river in England, and not to be confused with the Yorkshire Ouse, or with rivers of the same name elsewhere.

The Great Ouse, with its tributaries, the Claydon Brook and the Tow in Northamptonshire, the Lovat in Buckinghamshire, the Ivel in Bedfordshire, the Cam, Lark, Little Ouse and the Wessey

Fishing Fleet, King's Lynn

Pilot's Office, King's Lynn

in Cambridgeshire, and the Nar in Norfolk, drains 2,700 square miles of eastern England. It presented an engineering problem to generations, and has had untold wealth spent upon it: in return it makes this vast area of England pleasantly habitable for man.

Despite all this, the river has not flowed to fame. It has impressed few poets or painters; J M W Turner, in his younger days, made a sketch of the Bridge at Bedford; the Frazer Brothers produced a few later colours, but it has no-one approaching a Constable to portray it on canvas. In the realm of literature William Cowper is the only outstanding name to have connections; and, with the exception of Oliver Cromwell, the famous names in political history have passed it by.

However, it is a most attractive river; it wanders with unhurried pace through some beautiful scenery, with a pastoral setting for practically the whole of its length; a river of relaxation; in fact, to describe it one might well borrow Tennyson's lines:

> I come from haunts of coot and hern,
> I make a sudden sally,
> And sparkle out among the fern,
> To bicker down a valley.

At the point where the Great Ouse reaches the sea stands King's Lynn: a town whose life has been moulded by the history of a thousand years.

Formerly Bishop's Lynn, its ecclesiastical developers built churches, collegiate establishments and charitable institutions, then, as commercial prosperity increased, the now-famous flint-faced chequered Guild Hall. The increased business within the town is reflected in the two Market Places, for Wednesday and for Saturday; and also in the predominance of warehouses adjoining the docks. After the Reformation, and as the powers of the Bishops decreased, the name was changed to King's Lynn.

When King John visited the town in 1204 he granted its first Royal Charter. During the following century the trade of the port expanded rapidly, and, as early as 1271, the merchants of Lynn were conducting business with the Scandinavian countries. The impressive range of warehouses running along Saint Margaret's Lane were built for the traffic connected with this trade and date from the 15th century. Their opposite numbers, with whom they formed the Hanseatic League, used the warehouses in Lynn while the Lynn merchants had comparable buildings, which still stand in Bergen.

With the development of modern commercial enterprises and a network of modern roads, King's Lynn, being the nearest port to Birmingham and the industrial Midlands, is today a very busy town and port indeed.

INDEX